Business Policy

Business Policy

An Analytical Introduction

Second Edition

GEORGE LUFFMAN
STUART SANDERSON
EDWARD LEA
BRIAN KENNY

First published 1987
Reprinted 1988, 1989, 1990
Second edition first published 1991

Basil Blackwell Ltd
108 Cowley Road, Oxford, OX4 1JF, UK

Basil Blackwell, Inc.
3 Cambridge Center
Cambridge, Massachusetts 02142, USA

Library of Congress Cataloging in Publication Data
Business policy : an analytical introduction / George Luffman ... [et al.].—2nd
ed.
p. cm.
Includes index.
ISBN 0–631–18195–4 (alk. paper)
1. Strategic planning. I. Luffman, George A.
HD30.28.B86 1991
658.4'012—dc20
91–3376 CIP
British Library Cataloguing in Publication Data
A CIP catalogue record for this book is available from the British Library.

Typeset in 10 on 12 pt Times by TecSet Ltd, Wallington, Surrey.
Printed in Great Britain by T J Press Ltd., Padstow, Cornwall.
This book is printed on acid-free paper.

Contents

vi   Contents

Preface

This book is the result of teaching business policy, otherwise known as corporate strategy or strategic management, to approximately 5000 students over more than a decade, at undergraduate and postgraduate levels and on short courses to managers in industry. The content also benefits from consultancy assignments with organizations seeking help with strategic decision-making. Finally, the book is based on a wide range of research by the authors and on an understanding of what research is of relevance to the subject.

Traditionally, business policy teaching has focused on the needs of the postgraduate student, where maturity, previous academic achievement and often previous work experience have provided a sound basis for the assimilation of advanced, participative learning techniques such as those provided by the business-case method. Whatever the nature of the business problems presented, such students are often able to draw upon some particular aspects of their background in relating to the task of problem analysis, strategic evaluation and determination of corrective courses of action. However, in recent years the subject has been included on many undergraduate courses, and the business community has become more concerned to understand the changing environment within which it operates.

Business policy education relies heavily on the integrative approach which requires an application of interdisciplinary business skills and, ideally, should be introduced in the final stages of the study programme. However, it is often the case that the advanced specialist disciplines must, by practical necessity, be taught concurrently, and in spite of attempts to schedule case studies in a progressive manner, there will invariably be instances in the preliminary stages where the students' lack of appropriate conceptual knowledge and analytical techniques may seriously inhibit, if not totally nullify, the learning process. In this respect, we have selected and structured the contents with a view to alleviating this often inherent drawback and, thus, the text should be considered as an introduction to business policy. It does not itemize all appropriate research as this may tend to confuse the student who is new to the subject.

Finally, we would point out that there is no substitute for a wider reading incorporating the many excellent books and articles on business policy and corporate strategy to which we make reference from time to time in the text. We are also aware of the dangers of attempting to place case analysis into a rigid conceptual framework. The student is advised to treat on its merits each case with which he or she is confronted, and to regard the specific situational analysis as the key determinant.

In summary, therefore, we believe that this text will prove of value to students of business policy and/or corporate strategy on both postgraduate and undergraduate courses in the business studies area in general. In addition, it can prove a useful introduction to the subject for diploma students in management or in the many accounting and other professional courses in which there is a growing requirement for students to acquire a much broader appreciation of business practice. The book will also be of practical value to businessmen who are looking for a more systematic approach to their strategic decision-making process.

We would like to thank Bryan Lowes, of the University of Bradford Management Centre, for his helpful comments on chapter 7. Also, our thanks go to Peter Buckley for chapter 10. We would like to thank Sylvia Ashdown and others for deciphering what passed as handwriting. Thanks are also due to Tim Goodfellow and his colleagues for their contribution to the final text. Finally, we acknowledge those companies, students and researchers who have provided the inputs which have made this book possible.

PART 1
The Business Policy
Framework

1 Introduction to Business Policy

Introduction—Business Policy and the Strategy
Concept—Features of Strategic Decisions—The Task of
Business Policy Analysis

1.1 INTRODUCTION

It is difficult to believe that the big successful companies of today are not
going to be around in 20 or 30 years time. However, a brief review of the
past few decades is clear evidence that current success is no 'predictor' of
future success. Household names and blue-chip companies over the past 20
or 30 years have disappeared completely or been subsumed by other
companies. Smiths Crisps, Hoover, BSA, Alfred Herbert, Clarkson Holidays and Laker Airways were once leading companies, now fallen alto-
gether or much reduced in status. Dunlop and BTR provide a fascinating
contrast. In the mid-1960s both were in the tyre business, with Dunlop
being a large and successful company, and BTR small and relatively
unprofitable. Dunlop continued in the tyre business and, after years of low
profitability, was taken over by BTR who stopped tyre manufacturing,
diversified and became one of the largest and most successful UK
companies.

The problems facing companies are mainly the result of the increase in
the rate of change in the environment in which they operate and a failure to
adapt to such changes. Even for banks and building societies, where
change has taken place slowly, changes over the past few years have been
of such significance that a wholly different approach to the management of
the businesses is required.

A further problem, which is compounded by the rate of change, is the
size and cost of investment required in some businesses, for instance
chemicals. As plant size, and consequently cost, increases, the length of
time over which the company can expect returns may also increase.
However, changes in fashion, technology or other aspects of the business
may result in the plant becoming redundant earlier than expected. This

increases the risk involved in investing in new plant. Also, the number of products and range of markets now covered by large multinational firms increases the complexity of forecasting future trends.

The rate of change, the size of investment and the extension of product market scope are mainly responsible for creating a relatively new problem in the business environment, namely: are existing products sold to our existing customers going to be sufficient to enable us to continue in business? In the period up to the Second World War, change took place more slowly and business was on a much smaller scale, so that while there were business failures, the future was more easily identifiable.

1.2   BUSINESS POLICY AND THE STRATEGY CONCEPT

In order to explore the problems which result in success or failure for a company, it is necessary to begin by defining some terms. To students of business policy the wealth of terms used in texts on general management theory may, at first sight, seem confusing. 'Business policy', 'corporate strategy', 'corporate planning' and 'strategic management' seem to be used interchangeably, while the various component terms relating to strategy formulation are not always clearly defined.

Although the term 'business policy' remains in popular usage in academic circles, this title by definition fails to indicate the scope and level of activity covered by the subject area. A definition which takes in the full scope of management tasks at both corporate and functional levels is that of the 'strategy concept'. This has been defined as 'the pattern of objectives, purposes or goals and major policies and plans for achieving these goals, stated in such a way as to define what business the company is in or is to be in and the kind of company it is or is to be.'[1] The more recent term 'strategic management' has been defined as 'that set of decisions and actions which lead to the development of an effective strategy or strategies to help achieve corporate objectives.'[2]

Strategic decisions are thus those decisions that are concerned with the entire environment in which the firm operates, the whole of the resources and people who constitute the company and the interface between the two. Failure to match appropriately the firm's output to the environment can have devastating consequences.

In order to understand this relationship more clearly, a descriptive model of the firm is outlined in figure 1.1. As can be seen, the environment of the firm, although seemingly complex, particularly if a dynamic view is taken, can be broken down into a number of sub-environments. A possible danger is to treat each in isolation, as environmental change is often a complex of several sub-environments interacting with each other. However, for the the sake of analysis, they may be viewed separately. As

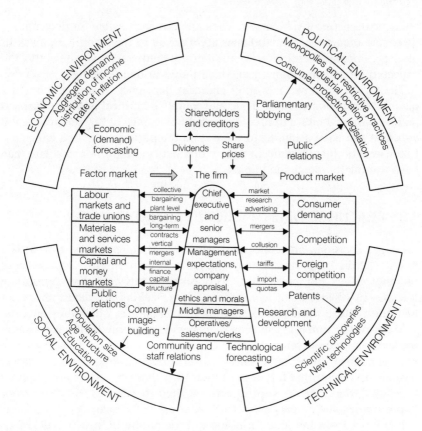

FIGURE 1.1 The firm: a descriptive model
Source: B. Lowes and J. R. Sparkes *Modern Managerial Economics*
(Heinemann, London 1974). Reprinted with permission.

will be stressed later, a firm rarely has the resources to scan and understand the total environment; rather, the firm has to decide on a hierarchy of what affects it most to what affects it least. This view will change over time, but the essence of strategic planning is to anticipate change, although any firm may not know the full extent of that change. For example, many oil companies may have known that the price of oil would eventually rise, but the problem was that none of them knew when or by exactly how much. This has led some critics to say that, as the environment is complex and the rate of change increasing, it is better to react than attempt to forecast and anticipate. While this option may be open for some companies, the problem is that any reaction may well mean that the company is too late and the strategic opportunity has gone.

In the centre of figure 1.1, within the firm, the chief executive and senior managers determine the management style and culture within which strategic decisions will be made. They are also responsible for determining corporate objectives and strategies appropriate to the resources and skills of the company in relation to the current and, more significantly, the expected future environment in which they will be operating.

The model as shown has one significant deficiency: it does not encompass the dimension of time. Time and timing are critical issues in business policy analysis. Failure to identify the rate of change of key environmental variables can have a significant impact on the performance of a company. Likewise, the introduction of a new product 'too early' or 'too late' can have a similarly damaging impact.

1.3   FEATURES OF STRATEGIC DECISIONS

Strategic decisions are concerned with the whole business, not with a division of the business or one of the functional areas. However, many of the approaches and analytical tools outlined in this book are appropriate for use by divisions of companies when seeking to determine their long-term future within the context of the company in which they operate.

Much of the time of operating managers is concerned with activities in the short or medium term, whereas corporate decisions are concerned with the long term. It is important, therefore, in a large, multidivisional business to ensure that for some of their time these managers are required to review the long-term prospects of their businesses so that major opportunities and threats are identified at an early stage.

It follows from the long-term and holistic nature of strategic decisions that they are almost always unique. That is, given that the environment changes and that the firm changes, the particular circumstances which surround a specific company at a point in time are different from those it faced five years ago or even last year, and because no two companies are identical in terms of management style, products, markets and resources, it is unlikely that experience from other companies will be of direct benefit. There are often similarities over time and between companies which provide the basis for analysis and comparison, but the differences are such and the regularity of strategic decisions so spread that, in comparison with other decisions, much greater uncertainty surrounds the outcome.

Strategic decisions are the point from which all other decisions and activities in the company emanate. They therefore provide direction and thus motivation: most people prefer to know the purpose and objectives of organizations to which they belong. It should be noted that 'to do nothing' is a strategic decision. To ignore information from the environment which might afford significant opportunities or threats is a decision 'to do nothing', even though the matter may not have been discussed at a board meeting or by senior managers.

It is the key role of strategic decision-making in the organization to integrate various activities within the company and to allocate resources. As part of the reason for a given set of resources and activities being combined to create a company is to gain maximum benefit from their interaction, it is important that all parts are working to the same ends, that there is no unnecessary conflict. Thus, integration and allocation become key outcomes of strategic decisions.

1.4 THE TASK OF BUSINESS POLICY ANALYSIS

It should be emphasized that a highly formalized system of planning is no guarantee of success but, equally, leaving things to chance constitutes the best possible guarantee of failure. The key to success is not so much in the adoption of a formal approach to strategy formulation per se, but rather in the quality and consistency of the implementation and in the organization's ability to adapt to an ever-changing business environment.

When students first begin a course in business policy they frequently express the view that they are not sure what it is they are supposed to do. Previously, their courses have been those of an information-giving nature, and it was understood that they should remember as much as they could and in addition 'read around' the subject to expand their understanding. Business policy as a course does not respond to this treatment. There is little to remember but much to apply. The student is required to adapt the normal learning patterns to the educational purpose of a business policy course. Generally, business policy is the educational course using material which business firms would title corporate strategy, but which in its educational setting aims to integrate features of the overall educational programme such as finance, marketing and organization behaviour. Understanding the inter-relationships between such activities enables the student to consider the corporate strategy of a business organization.

Therefore, the task of the student is to:

1 Understand the position of the company with respect to its internal strengths and weaknesses, and the opportunities and threats which emerge from an analysis of its external environment.
2 Bring to bear other knowledge (such as that gained from economics or finance) relevant to the strategic steps the company could take.
3 Evaluate the feasibility of strategic options.
4 Select from among the options and persuasively argue why the company should follow the selected path.

How to handle a case study is dealt with in our *Cases in Business Policy*. It is necessary to point out here that the role of the student is not to remember and learn facts about the firm, but to understand the current position of the company and the strategic moves available to such firms in such situations and then to be able to evaluate those moves.

Educationally, the purpose is a thorough understanding of strategy and its implications, for example, setting objectives, formulating strategy, implementing strategy and considering the feasibility of such steps and the level of risks associated with them. This is done in such a way that at the end the student can understand the process of strategic thinking in a company, the constraints upon that process (for instance, the environment and the company itself) and the problems of implementation and achievement.

It is also important to add that the text is not about how to undertake 'corporate planning', which is a management process involving much greater application of techniques. Argenti, Jones and others provide adequate coverage of this topic.[3]

NOTES

1   Edmund P. Learned, C. Roland Christensen, Kenneth Andrews and William D. Guth, *Business Policy: Text and Cases* (Richard D. Irwin Inc., Homewood, Ill., 1965).
2   W. F. Glueck, *Business Policy and Strategic Management* (McGraw-Hill, New York, 1980).
3   See John Argenti, *Systematic Corporate Planning* (Wiley, New York, 1974); Harry Jones, *Preparing Company Plans: a Workbook for Effective Corporate Planning* (2nd edn, Gower, Aldershot, 1983).

2 Strategic Managers and Strategic Planning

Strategic Managers—The Strategic Planning
Model—Corporate Planning

2.1 STRATEGIC MANAGERS

In the previous chapter the nature and extent of strategic decisions were examined. It is now appropriate to consider who has the responsibility for making these decisions and how that responsibility is discharged in practice. As strategic decisions are concerned with the direction of the whole of the company in the long term, they are clearly the responsibility of the chief executive and the board of directors.

Functions of the Board

The board of directors is appointed or elected by the shareholders to manage the assets in the interests of the shareholders by:

- ensuring the long-term success of the company through attention to the mission, objectives, strategies and policies of the company;
- disseminating such information to appropriate stakeholders;
- reviewing and publishing at regular intervals the financial performance of the company;
- employing appropriate senior personnel to achieve these tasks;
- reviewing periodically the organizational structure of the organization to ensure implementation of the plan.

A key question is to what extent a board of directors actually has any power? It has been suggested that boards are best described as decision-taking, rather than decision-making, institutions. In many cases there is no doubt that senior management engage in manipulative strategies with the aim of getting proposals through the board by giving only generalized estimates of costs involved and minimum expectations of outcomes. The key resides in the power of the senior management to control information.

Provided no contrary information is placed before the board, it is often difficult to object to proposals. These tactics require effort at pre-board meetings to prepare the cases and often summaries of board papers so that the board can digest them at one sitting.

Membership of the Board

First of all there is the chairman. It appears that the chairman may be an executive or non-executive chairman. In the latter case the chairman would only be employed part time in the company and there would also be a chief executive officer (CEO) whose title may be CEO or managing director. Thomas Risk (chairman of the Royal Bank of Scotland), when it was proposed that he be non-executive chairman of the newly formed Guinness after the takeover of Distillers, said 'in company law there is only a chairman.' That is, executive and non-executive have nothing to do with it. So, is the non-executive chairman merely a figurehead who only presides at meetings or someone who does not assume direct responsibility for managing any specific part of the company but who nevertheless retains overall responsibility for the results?

In the industrialized West there are basically three types of board:

1   In Britain there is a unitary (or single) board which is mostly comprised of executive directors.
2   In the USA the board is unitary but mostly non-executive.
3   West Germany has a two-tier board system in which there is a wholly non-executive supervisory board and a wholly executive management board with no members in common.

There are a number of objections which can be made about the British system where executive directors:

- may be excessively preoccupied with their own day-to-day problems and may give priority to their own responsibilities;
- may spend an inordinate time using the board to negotiate resources for their own area of responsibility;
- cannot be expected to make judgements on their own performance;
- are not likely to sack themselves should the need arise.

In this sense a fully executive board is constitutionally incapable of performing many of the tasks it is responsible for and is probably no more than a management committee.

There are arguments against the two-tier system. A letter to *The Financial Times* on 17 April 1989 from Mr Ralph Instone read as follows:

Sir, If we are to have two-tier boards, as proposed by Mr Edgar Palamountain (letters, April 22), it will be necessary to define the matters on which the non-executive directors must pronounce.

Is their opinion to be required only in the case of resisted bids, management buy outs, and other changes where a conflict of interest may arise? If so, it would be far simpler for the City Panel to require the circulation of a reasoned opinion from non-executive directors in all such operations above a certain size. But consistency would require a similar opinion in the case of all acquisitions and other transactions needing shareholders' approval.

The trouble with this approach is that non-executive directors can only second guess the views of management and its advisers, presumably on the basis of the same evidence which had already satisfied the management. Does anyone suppose that a non-executive committee of the Blue Arrow board, for example, would have pronounced against the acquisition of Manpower?

The improvement of managerial judgement and performance will not be secured by a division of functions between executive and non-executive directors; still less by changes in the law.

Non-executive Directors

1   What is their role?

- They should bring independence and objectivity to the board. Subordinate managers will always find it difficult to speak openly in front of their immediate superiors.
- They can provide specialist advice or skills, e.g. a knowledge of government procurement.
- They can form special committees, e.g. a compensation committee.

2   What proportion should be non-executive?

- More than is currently the case at the present time; for example Tootal 3/9, M&S 0/15.

3   What qualities and qualifications should they have?

- Credibility is important and so is the time to commit themselves to the company, e.g. two days per month at least.

4   How are they appointed?

It has usually been the case that they are appointed by the chairman and ratified at the annual general meeting (AGM). Increasingly, boards are setting up nomination committees made up of non-executive directors to

give advice to the chairman. This prevents the constant appointment of
friends. However, it does not help the situation where there are no
non-executive directors in the first place.

Sir Owen Green, chairman of BTR, has said that non-executive
directors with no particular experience of a company do not have enough
information to make a real contribution. According to Allen Shephard,
chairman of Grand Metropolitan, non-executive directors do not need a
detailed knowledge of the business. Their role is to ask the right questions
rather than to know all the answers. Their most valuable contribution has
to do with strategy: does what the executives say about the future sound
beliveable? For Ian McLaurin, chairman of Tesco, an important role for the
non-executive is in telling the chief executive when it is time to step down.

Responsibility and Accountability

Under UK law a director of a company is both individually and jointly with
the other directors accountable for the company's viability and success, i.e.
for its satisfactory performance. Whereas a manager shares responsibility,
each director's responsibility is for the whole company. So the director is
accountable to the company (which is a legal body), and the directors also
have a fiduciary responsibility to the shareholders of the company, i.e.
acting on their behalf.

Strictly speaking, the shareholders of a company own neither the
company nor its assets; they own shares and these convey certain rights
upon them. Similarly, directors are not servants of the shareholders. Their
responsibility is to the company. Nevertheless, the authority of the board
stems from the powers entrusted to it by the shareholders, in return for
which the board undertakes to protect the interests of the shareholders.

If shareholders disagree with the decision of the board they cannot
change the decision. They can, however, remove the directors at the next
AGM. For example, if the directors propose a certain dividend payment
the shareholders cannot increase it.

Company law has prescribed the extent to which a director is accountable for his actions. In 1986, the Insolvency Act extended these responsibilities by making a director liable for a 'wrongful act' which is a stage further
than a fraudulent act and which can lead to claims against a director. This
has led to directors seeking a legal indemnity clause in their contracts when
they resign and to directors taking out insurance policies against any
damages awarded.

Where a board makes a decision with which a director disagrees
(especially if it involves an illegal act), then the director cannot escape
responsibility by voting against the proposal or by having his or her
opposition noted in the minutes. If he or she cannot prevent the decision
and does not agree with it, then the only recourse is to resign.

Companies legislation says that it is unlawful for a company to make any payment to a director by way of compensation for loss of office, or as a consideration for his retirement, without particulars of the proposed payment, including the amount, being disclosed to and approved by the shareholders. However, this does not apply to any bona fide payment by way of damages for breach of contract or by way of pension in respect of past services.

A board of directors has statutory requirements with respect to a wide variety of issues such as financial management and reporting, health and safety, product quality and reliability, pollution emission levels and so on. The extent of liability is constantly being tested in the courts and is consequently changing regularly.

The directors' discharge of both their statutory obligations and their management of shareholders' funds has been the subject of much research. In one recent survey of executives it was found that in only 25 per cent of businesses did the board have any significant impact on the strategic success of their organizations. Nethertheless, by whoever or however the strategy is formulated, if the result is poor the board of directors will be held responsible.

2.2   THE STRATEGIC PLANNING MODEL

We saw in chapter 1 that few organizations operate in circumstances where the rate of change is so slow that there is no need to consider the future on the basis that what is currently being produced and sold is likely to provide a formula for success in the long term. It follows, therefore, that some evaluation process is necessary. Thus, whatever the size of the company, it needs to develop a strategic perspective. This might be achieved through a formal planning system, especially if the company is large with many markets and products to evaluate and/or where the rate of change is rapid. A strategic perspective could be achieved through the skill and experience of one person, although the evidence of the success of this mode of decision-making over the long term is not good. Indeed, the major factor evident in corporate collapse is 'the one man band' (see chapter 12).

In the short term, results based on the intuition and knowledge of one person can often be spectacular (for example, George Davies and Next), but it is often difficult to sustain such success over the long term and, whether or not it is successful, the resignation, retirement or death of these individuals often leaves a large vacuum as there has rarely been any attention focused on management development and succession.

The model outlined in this book has been described as the rational analytical model and is that most widely taught in business schools and used by departments charged with the responsibility for developing a strategic perspective often labelled strategic or corporate planning. Most practitioners have their own modifications but few vary from the basic model which follows any problem-solving situation:

- awareness of the problem;
- exploration of the problem;
- deciding what to do;
- taking action to implement the decision;
- examination and feedback of results.

A comprehensive picture of the process as it applies to strategic decisions is outlined in figure 2.1.

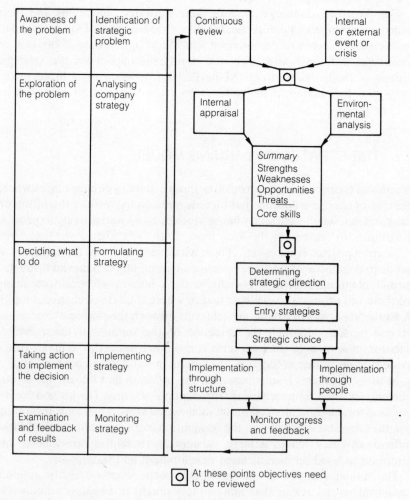

FIGURE 2.1   The strategic decision-making process

The simplified model contains the major features of the process and represents the structure of this book. Each chapter in parts II–V is preceded by this diagram with an indicator identifying the section of the model to which the chapter refers. It is hoped that this will enable readers to understand the comprehensive nature of the process. Thus, part II, 'Strategic Analysis', is concerned with evaluating the current strategic position of the company in relation to its environment. From this analysis, which summarizes strengths, weaknesses, opportunities and threats (SWOT), the next stage is to identify possible strategies and this is the focus of part III, 'Identifying Strategic Alternatives'. Having identified possible options, it is then necessary to make some choices and part IV, 'Strategic Choice', provides some frameworks which are useful for this purpose. Finally, part V, 'Implementing Company Strategy', is concerned with getting the choice implemented and monitoring and feeding back the results.

Whether the strategic thinking is done on the back of an envelope by one person, or through a formal planning process, these are the necessary steps in the thought process.

2.3   CORPORATE PLANNING

The means by which the strategic decision-making process is pursued is outlined in the subsequent chapters of the book but some preliminary comments are appropriate with respect to two matters: the inter-relationship of planning at different levels of the business, and the planning cycle and organization.

Hofer and Schendel have differentiated between three major levels of organizational strategy.[1] These are at the corporate, business and functional levels respectively (see figure 2.2). The category of 'corporate strategy' occupies the highest level of strategic decision-making and, in comparative terms, would relate to the multidivisional organization or the firm with a wide range of business interests. Such decisions might include high-level finanacial policy, acquisition and divestment, diversification and organizational structure.

At the 'business' level the respective decision-makers are more concerned with the immediate industry/product–market issues and the harnessing together of the individual functional units in the most efficient manner. New product development and market segmentation will play a primary role in decision-making, along with the major policy areas across the spectrum of production, R&D, personnel and finance.

Functional strategy, as is suggested by its title, relates to a single functional operation and the activities involved therein. Decisions at this level within the organization are often described as 'tactical', but it should

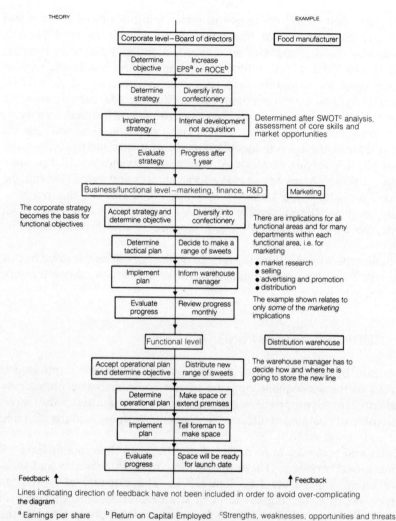

FIGURE 2.2   Strategy implications at different levels

be noted that such decisions ought always to be guided and constrained by some overall strategic consideration. For example, product diversification decisions will need to be considered within the overall framework of business strategy, although what products are actually decided upon will be at the discretion of the marketing specialist, given that the investment is approved (finance) and that the appropriate production facilities (manufacturing) and manpower (personnel) are or will be available.

It is important that the implications of strategic decisions made by the board of directors are identified and implemented at all levels in the firm.

At the operational level, there are actions which need to be taken if the objective from which the policy stems is to be realized. Even at this level, failure to have a fully integrated plan could have serious consequences.

Accepting this hierarchical nature of strategy, it will be appreciated that objectives and policies can be established for the three tiers of managerial responsibility discussed. Formal goals and objectives provide the means by which the organization's performance can be evaluated and, if necessary, adjusted in the face of environmental change. Similarly, the process allows for the allocation of resources in a more formalized manner and in keeping with planning effectiveness, monitoring and control.

Although this book is not focused on the nuts and bolts of the corporate planning process in businesses, an outline of a few of the issues is considered relevant. A significant issue is the determination of the planning cycle. That is, the process and times by which information will be available, so that decisions have been made before the start of the planning period. Organization for planning is also important: who should be involved, to what degree and how will the various actions of the different participants in the process be coordinated? How much information is needed and who is going to produce it are other key issues, as is the regularity with which the strategic plan should be updated.

Perhaps the most important point to emphasize is that *planning must be a dialogue* between directors and subordinates or head office and divisions. Too much 'top-down' or 'bottom-up' planning is liable to render the process ineffective. *Meaningful dialogue with realistic, not over-optimistic or over-pessimistic, plans is the only recipe for successful planning.*

NOTE

1   Charles W. Hofer and Dan Schendel, *Strategy Formulation: Analytical Concepts* (West Publishing Co, St Paul, Minnesota, 1978).

3 Values, Culture and Power

Introduction—Values and Culture—Culture and Strategy
Formulation—Strategic Performance and Culture—Culture
and Organization—Power—Management Summary and
Checklist

3.1 INTRODUCTION

An understandable misperception of many people approaching strategic
management for the first time is that a strategic planning system is in itself
sufficient to ensure that the right questions are posed, a correct analysis is
performed and suitable strategies are developed. In reality, such a view
ignores the basic fact that the systems themselves do none of these
tasks – they are performed by people. Thus, realistically, organizations
make strategic responses to a changing environment through people, either
individually or collectively. It would compound the perception further if
the people part of the strategic equation were seen as the complicating
factor; rather, it should be regarded as the reality of the situation. The
purpose of this chapter, therefore, is to provide an initial insight into
important aspects of these individual and collective behavioural dimensions of the strategic process.

3.2 VALUES AND CULTURE

Many readers will probably be familiar with workplace phrases such as 'the
way we do things here', 'it's not the sort of business we want to get into',
'we are different here' and so on. Such statements are often manifestations of the values and culture held by the organization and as such are
powerful determinants of how an organization behaves. Further, on a
macro level, there has been much debate of late in terms of national
cultures and their effect on industrial prosperity.

Culture is a major determinant of managerial perceptions, which in turn affects recruitment, resource allocation and management, and organizational design – indeed, all aspects of an organization. Utilizing the McKinset Seven–S framework, the relationship is shown in figure 3.1.

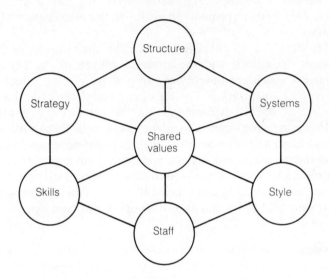

FIGURE 3.1   The McKinsey Seven–S framework
Source: R. H. Waterman, T. J. Peters and J. R. Phillips 'Structure is not Organisation', Business Horizons, June 1980, pp. 14–26. Reprinted with permission.

Shared values have been termed superordinate goals (incremental) but essentially are sets of values and aspirations which underpin objective statements and as such are fundamental to and deep seated within the organization. Whether formally expressed or not, they are omnipresent and often drive the other six 'S' in the framework.

3.3   CULTURE AND STRATEGY FORMULATION

Several researchers have identified typologies of culture and their effect upon strategic decision-making. Mintzberg and others have identified entrepreneurial, adaptive and planning organizations.[1] Entrepreneurial organizations tend to be characterized by growth, the search for new opportunities, with power held by the chief executive. Such organizations often exhibit dramatic change.

Organizations without clear explicit objectives tend to exhibit adaptive strategies which are often a function of conflicting goals held by senior managers. In this way they react to environmental change and decisions tend to be incremental and based upon the power conflicts in the organization, resulting in fragmented strategic decisions. Planning organizations are characterized by coordinated anticipatory decision-making which results in a number of scenarios about the future with differing strategies. This tends to promote the value to the organization of analysis and analysts.

Clearly, there is a relationship between the environment in which the organization finds itself and the strategic culture of the organization. Environments which are developing are perhaps more conducive to the entrepreneurial organization. Volatile environments may suit the adaptive mode, whereas stable environments may be conducive to the planning mode. However, much care should be taken with the above as multi-product, multi-market organizations may face different types of environment and thus many modes may be apparent in any organization.

Other researchers have attempted to classify organizations in relation to their behaviour, stemming from their culture and strategic responses over time. For example, Miles and Snow identified four typologies.[2]

Defenders   tend to be conservative, well-tried ideas, low risk;
Prospecters   immature, higher risk, seek market opportunities;
Analysers   strong on monitoring strategy, formal structures;
Reacters   find it difficult to adapt, crisis management.

In this way it can be seen that, faced with a similar problem, different organizations will respond differently. For example, faced with a decline in turnover, the defender will seek to cut costs to restore margins, 'batten down the hatches'; the prospecter will look for new markets and opportunities; the analyser will spend time looking for reasons before changing, but may well have anticipated the change; the reactor will do something about it when it begins to hurt.

Research by Grinyer and Spender has shown that a manifestation of culture in many organizations' strategic decision-making is the creation of 'recipes'.[3] These tend to be strongly held beliefs and ideas about what works. As such, they are responses to a changing environment which are perceived to have worked well in the past and are thus embedded in the organization. They are frequently not questioned, as to do so often results in an attack on the superordinate goals held by an organization which are manifest in the values of senior managers who attained their position via such recipes. Like many cultural aspects of an organization, they create a perceptive framework which focuses senior managers' views of the environment and the organization and can act as a constraint on strategic action.

3.4   STRATEGIC PERFORMANCE AND CULTURE

Given the nature of the relationship between culture and strategy, several enquirers have attempted to discover what relationships exist between performance and culture. Deal and Kennedy, researching American companies, found that successful companies (above-average long-term performance) were those who believed in something which permeated the whole organization.[4] They further argue that in addition to endemic beliefs, employees ought to be rewarded for behaviour which complies with such belief. In essence, the major aspects of culture which appear to contribute towards success are seen to be a close relationship between critical success factors and values, which are well communicated such that they become institutionalized as rituals in the organization. They are often implanted by visionary managers who set the culture. Strong cultures can assist in prioritizing problems and providing a framework for what is expected of people.

Other insights into the relationship between culture and performance are provided by Peters and Waterman in their book *In Search of Excellence*.[5] While the book has suffered some academic criticism and some of the then excellent companies in their sample would no longer qualify, the book and subsequent work by the authors have provided interesting notions about success and culture. Peters and Waterman indentified eight characteristics of excellence as follows:

- a bias for action
- close to the customer
- autonomy and entrepreneurship
- hands-on value driven
- stick to the knitting
- simple form lean staff
- simultaneous loose–tight properties.

Peters and Waterman's work has been a catalyst for a number of books in the area, for example *The Winning Streak* by Goldsmith and Clutterbuck,[6] but care must be taken in using the findings for there is a danger that the findings are themselves used as a recipe for success. If business was that simple, then everybody would be doing it. This raises the issue of, first, what are successful cultures and, secondly, whether or not successful cultures can be transplanted or initiated to improve corporate performance. The limiting factors on such a proposition stem often from difficulties in defining culture, the receptivity of organizations to new cultures and the time it takes to implement cultural change. It is perhaps easier to change culture when something serious has happened to a company; for example, a loss or an unwelcome takeover bid. These may be described as short, sharp shocks. However, the more incremental methods of cultural change, which inevitably occur and indeed have to occur, often take longer, for any organization is a function of its history, and cultural change has to take place, first, by a recognition that what is currently in place is inappropriate and, secondly, by defining what should take its place.

3.5 CULTURE AND ORGANIZATION

Organizational effectiveness is a fundamental concept in strategic planning. Aspects of organizational design are dealt with in chapter 15; at this point it suffices to discuss the relationship between organizations and culture.

Handy has provided a framework for explaining this relationship by defining four types of culture found in organizations: power, role, task and person.[7]

Power   These tend to be organizations with strong central authority with few rules. Typically entrepreneurial, high risk, run by powerful individuals.

Role   Less personality run, more bureaucratic, well-defined roles, system and procedures, more risk averse.

Task   Problem-solving dominates, relies heavily on expertise and teamwork, personality less important. Often results in a matrix.

Person   Based on serving the needs of individual members. Evident in professional organizations such as lawyers. Can be found in other three typologies. Often difficult to manage individuals as individuals may not be responsible to personal or expert power.

As can be seen from the above, Handy's typologies have a lot to do with power in organizations which can be a manifestation of the structure, the effect of coalitions or the personality of the entrepreneur.

3.6 POWER

Power is essentially the ability to engage in action and as such is important in attempting to effect strategic change. Power has both internal and external implications. The discussion of external power is left to further chapters; the emphasis in this chapter will be confined to its internal aspects.

Any discussion of power in organizations has to take account of further concepts of authority and control. Power has a contextual or relationship circumstance. For example, authority is the final power vested in specific roles or positions in an organization; often it is delegated from the top and thus the amount of authority a manager has may well depend on how much the chief executive is willing to delegate. Clearly, there may be advantages in a marriage of power and authority within an organization and many systems such as rewards are geared to such a union, but often they can be divorced from each other, particularly in terms of informal power relationships. Informal power can occur because of expertise or specialization, historical evidence of being right, clear use of internal politics or a host of other reasons. Strategically, the problem is that if power groups become dominant, then they could affect or halt necessary strategic change. It is often useful to revisit major decisions to examine the extent of the power which influenced such decisions. A continuing problem in many organizations is that powerful people control those systems whereby others gain power, and thus people get to the top because they adhere to the values of the dominant power group, thus negating the alternative view or indeed a better approach.

3.7 MANAGEMENT SUMMARY AND CHECKLIST

In this chapter an attempt has been made to introduce the reader to important behavioural dimensions of the strategic process. In essence, the proposition is that organizations do not respond to environmental change; it is people who do. Thus the effects of culture, values, power and authority have a large effect on strategy formulation and success. Discovering values in an organization is not easy for the consultant or analyst; a number of questions have to be posed, answers analysed and behaviour observed to come to a view. It is, however, for the senior manager an important aspect of the role, for culture and values do change and often have to change, thus they have to be managed, which in turn means they have to be understood in a strategic setting.

Values and culture

1   What 'cultural' statements are made by senior executives?
2   To what extent have major decisions been influenced by the culture?
3   Would you classify the company as a defender or a prospecter?
4   What are attitudes to risk – why?
5   Would you classify the company as entrepreneurial, adaptive or planning – why?

6   What do you think the dominant values are – where did they come from?
7   What evidence is there for Peters and Waterman's characteristics of excellence?
8   How would you define the organization's culture in terms of Charles Handy's classification?
9   Has the company a strong strategic recipe?

Power

1   Who has the power in the organization?
2   What are the bases of such power?
3   In reviewing decisions taken in the organization, who made them?
4   What are the attitudes of middle managers to senior managers?
5   If you have an alternative view of the company and its strategy, how easy do you think it would be to get people to listen to you?

NOTES

1   H. Mintzberg, 'Strategy Making in Three Modes', *California Management Review* 16, no. 2 (1973), pp. 44–53.
2   R. E. Miles and C. C. Snow, *Organisation Strategy, Structure and Process* (McGraw-Hill, New York, 1978).
3   P. H. Grinyer and J-C. Spender, 'Recipes, Crises and Adaptation in Mature Business', *International Studies of Management and Organisation*, 19, no. 3 (1979) p. 113.
4   T. Deal and A. Kennedy, *Corporate Cultures, the Rites and Rituals of Corporate Life* (Addison Wesley, London, 1982).
5   T. J. Peters and R. H. Waterman Jr, *In Search of Excellence: Lessons from America's Best Run Companies* (Harper & Row, New York, 1982).
6   W. Goldsmith and D. Clutterbuck, *The Winning Streak* (Weidenfeld and Nicolson, London, 1984).
7   C. Handy, *Understanding Organisations* (Penguin, Harmondsworth, 1976).

4 Mission and Objectives

4.1 INTRODUCTION

According to an old saying, 'If you don't know where you are going, you cannot get lost.' This is perhaps of comfort to some managers but the proposition developed in previous chapters is that strategic planning is a conscious process of decision-making about the future, which involves the creation of purposeful strategies. It may be possible to think about the future without objectives, but the deployment of meaningful strategies necessitates some ends (objectives) against which means (strategies) are developed.

There has been much debate regarding the nature of objectives, for example, long versus short term, financial versus non-financial, the distinction between strategy and objectives, as well as how and who is responsible for setting them.

It is perhaps useful to distinguish between types of objectives – those concerned with broad aims and purposes and those that are quantifiable and measurable, both in the long and short run. The former tend to pose questions about what the organization is and wants to be, while the latter set specific targets for evaluation and act as control mechanisms on how well the organization is achieving its broad purpose.

4.2 MISSION

Missions tend to be about broad purposes. They often contain elements of long-term strategy as well as desired outcomes. What they often reflect are the basic values and philosophy of the organization as perceived by the senior managers who write them.

Practices regarding their dissemination appear to differ; some are actively published to the environment, some seem to be confined within the company and communicated to all personnel, some targeted to senior staff. In large companies with major strategic business units, there may be different mission statements for each subsidiary. The underlying rationale for developing and disseminating mission statements is that they act as visionary and motivating statements but also legitimize the organization in terms of what the dominant values are, why it exists, what types of businesses it will be in and what its subsequent behaviour will be.

Mission statements have been criticized for being so vaguely written that they could be applicable to any organization, also they have been termed 'motherhood' statements with commentators saying 'Well you would say that, wouldn't you?'. They appear to be effective when the successful behaviour of an organization both reflects and emanates the mission statement.

4.3   EXAMPLES OF MISSION STATEMENTS

Marks & Spencer

To offer our customer a selected range of goods of high quality and good value.

To work in close cooperation with our suppliers to develop this catalogue.

Always to buy British providing the goods the British suppliers produce represent good quality and good value.

To develop and maintain good human relations with our staff, our suppliers and our customers.

Trust House Forte

To increase profitability and earnings per share each year in order to encourage investment and to improve and expand the business.

To give complete customer satisfaction by efficient and courteous service, with value for money.

To support managers and their staff in using personal initiative to improve the profit and quality of their operations while observing the company's policies.

To provide good working conditions and to maintain effective communications at all levels to develop better understanding and assist decision-making.

To ensure no discrimination against sex, race, colour or creed and to train, develop and encourage promotion within the company based on merit and ability.

To act with integrity at all times and to maintain a proper sense of responsibility towards the public.

To recognize the importance of each and every employee who contributes towards these aims.

4.4 OBJECTIVES

The debate surrounding objectives has been joined by many with differing views. Economic theory states that the firm should attempt to maximize profits. The proposition provides a useful starting point, but it has been criticized from a number of viewpoints, leading to reformulations of the goals of the firm by people such as Baumol, who proposed the goal of sales maximization and various others suggesting growth models. Rather than extend this debate, what is of interest here is where do objectives come from, what is their purpose and what is their nature?

4.5 SOURCES

All organizations have to take into account the demands of the environment when setting objectives. The needs of the environment are complex and can result in conflicting objectives for an organization. The needs of the environment and the organization can perhaps be encapsulated by viewing such demands as pressures from stakeholders.

An organization's stakeholders	Needs and interests
Shareholders or owners	Income flows, capital appreciation
Suppliers	Continued success of the company
Customers	Quality products at preferred prices
Employees	Salaries, wages, employment
Government	Taxes, contribution to GNP
Society	Environmental issues, consumer concerns, pollution

The above represents certain key stakeholders and some of their aspirations. Against these one has to set the values and aspirations of senior managers whose personal 'stake' will affect objective setting, remembering that such managers may be shareholders.

Additionally, the interests of the various stakeholders can appear to pull organizations in differing ways. A method of dealing with this conflict may be to deal with each; sequentially, this is difficult, if not dangerous. Prioritizing objectives into some form of hierarchy may assist, particularly in terms of strategic decision-taking, but for most organizations there will often be an overriding goal of profitability. In a real sense the aspirations of all stakeholders cannot be met unless the company is profitable. Clearly, a distinction has to be made for not-for-profit organizations, and these are dealt with separately below.

Profitability is arguably different from the economists' initial notions of profit maximization for companies in a real world of imperfect information. It is somewhat doubtful if people maximize their behaviour, preferring to satisfy, i.e. attain satisfactory performance. Additionally, there is a continuing debate as to whether organizations can have objectives separately from the objectives of senior people within them.

4.6   OBJECTIVES AND STRATEGY

Many organizations will state their objectives in terms such as 'a certain percentage market share', 'good-quality products', 'a happy and well-rewarded workforce' and so on. The question arises as to whether these are objectives or strategies. It is easy, for example, in a price-sensitive market, to increase market share by dropping prices, but profits may disappear. There is, too, the danger that a function of a company might read its own agenda into market-share growth and set off doing things to the detriment of the organization. Such statements on their own are probably means to an end rather than the end in themselves. When stated along with profitability targets they act as constraints on the achievement of financial objectives.

4.7   THE NATURE OF OBJECTIVES

A prime purpose of objectives is to set targets or benchmarks against which performance can be measured. Thus to be of worth to an organization, objectives should be:

- measurable
- achievable
- realistic

- explicit
- internally consistent with each other
- communicable to others.

In many organizations there will be a hierarchy of objectives, as below

MISSION
↓
STRATEGIC OBJECTIVES – SENIOR MANAGERS
↓
TACTICAL OBJECTIVES – MIDDLE MANAGERS
↓
OPERATIONAL OBJECTIVES – SUPERVISORS
AND JUNIOR MANAGERS

They ideally 'fit' together in that senior managers' decisions create the domain within which middle managers set their objectives. Each level has, however, specific concerns, and the role of senior managers is to articulate objectives which create consensus amongst stakeholders, whereas the role of middle managers is often concerned with implementing strategy and setting functional objectives.

4.8   NOT-FOR-PROFIT ORGANIZATIONS

A major problem for not-for-profit organizations is the apparent lack of a single discipline against which to set objectives, as for example profit. Like companies, they have a multiplicity of objectives but they are often difficult to reconcile. Thus, such organizations can end up with objectives which appear to be qualitative rather than quantitative, conflicting, complex and difficult to measure. Further, stakeholders may exert an important influence on the objectives.

Thus performance is difficult to measure. Just what constitutes a good not-for-profit organization is often a matter of debate. For example, what constitutes a good museum, art gallery, school or hospital? The satisfaction of the stakeholders, while attractive, may be difficult to achieve, for often such stakeholders are difficult to define and their needs are conflicting. A temptation is to deal with them sequentially or prioritize according to the strength of their needs. Often, surrogate measures are used, such as number of visitors, patients or examination pass rates, but these are often conditional on other external parameters.

Perhaps the answer is to measure what you can, but to be confident that the correct measure is being used in terms of stakeholders. This probably necessitates a greater knowledge of stakeholder aspirations.

4.9 MANAGEMENT SUMMARY AND CHECKLIST

Objectives are essentially a matter for any organization in terms of the levels or rates of performance they describe. However, in the case of companies, it is difficult to escape those financial objectives by which the market measures their performance. The visibility of a company's financial performance is now a major strategic concern for senior managers who have to spend time 'talking to the City'.

The process by which organizations set objectives is also a senior management concern as it affects motivation, morale and the ownership of targets by managers. The process tends to be iterative in that organizations will discuss objectives in terms of company competencies and the external environment, which are the subject of subsequent chapters.

1   Does the organization have a set of explicit objectives?
2   To what extent are the stated objectives achievable?
3   How do the stated objectives fit with past behaviour?
4   Do the objectives fit the stated strategy?
5   In what terms are the objectives stated: long term, short term, financial, non-financial?
6   Do the objectives give any indication of the organization's attitudes to profits in the long and short term?
7   Are the objectives and mission the result of dominant stakeholder opinion?
8   To what extent are the mission and objectives the result of the power of a senior manager or a dominant coalition?
9   Does the mission statement have any operational meaning?

PART II
Strategic Analysis

5 Environmental Analysis

Introduction—The Environment of the Firm—Strategic
Posture—Environmental Forecasting—Management Summary
and Checklist

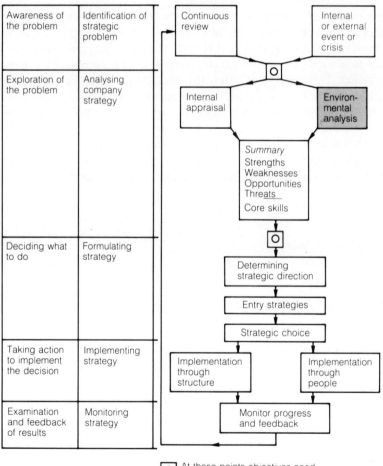

FIGURE 5.1   The strategic decision-making process

5.1   INTRODUCTION

Environmental change is one of the major influences upon the performance of business (and other) organizations, and at the same time largely
beyond the control of the management of the organization. It is no
accident that managers refer to a 'turbulent environment' within which
they have to manage.

For some companies the environment is more turbulent than for others,
as some (such as tobacco companies) may find themselves in a situation
where everything appears hostile; for instance, a product in long-term
decline due to health factors, government actions on taxation and advertising, and increasing social disapproval.

It is important, therefore, to have some way of screening the environment surrounding a company, the changes operating within it and the
consequential opportunities and threats posed to that company. To the
extent that these are in the future, then it can be considered a form of
forecasting. However, it is often the case that it is sufficient to gather
together and analyse the trends already apparent within that environment.

A framework is presented in figure 5.2 which can be used to prepare an
overview of the factors influencing the company at the time, the changes
currently under way (trends) and the potential implications of these. As
the industry within which the organization finds itself is considered
important, then part of this framework (industry structure) is examined in

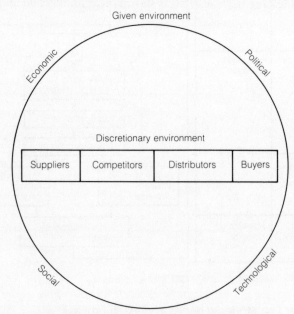

FIGURE 5.2   The firm and its environments

more detail in chapter 6 as it is usually of critical importance to the company.

Figure 5.2 differs from the model of the organization and its environment shown in chapter 1 in that it makes the distinction between those environments in which a company has some discretion and those where it has little. A company can do little about the general state of politics, economics etc., but it does have some discretion over who it buys from and sells to. At the same time, however, any company must realize that the nature and dynamics of the discretionary environment is a function of the wider or given environment. It should be remembered that, although for planning purposes the given environment cannot be directly influenced, companies and organizations can alter their sensitivities to this environment via their strategic decision-making; for example, by choice of country to manufacture in and types of technology to use. However, once these choices are made, the new environment acts as a 'given' in the planning process.

For the organization, the task of environmental scanning is twofold: first, to isolate these environmental variables to which the organization is sensitive and, secondly, to collect data in order to understand the trends in these selected variables. There is not, unfortunately, an easy way of accomplishing the first task. It is essentially a matter of 'learning' by examining the effects of the environment upon the attainment of objectives. Essentially, it is a process of prioritizing environmental variables in terms of the likelihood of certain things happening and their consequent effect upon the organization. This is shown diagrammatically in figure 5.3.

		High	High	Medium
	High	High priority	High priority	Medium priority
Probability of occurrence	Medium	High priority	Medium priority	Low priority
	Low	Medium priority	Low priority	Low priority
		High	Medium	Low

Probable impact on corporation

FIGURE 5.3   Issues priority matrix
Source: L. L. Lederman, 'Foresight Activities in the USA: Time for a Reassessment,' Journal of Long Range Planning (June 1984), p. 46, Pergamon Journals Ltd. Reprinted with permission.

5.2   THE ENVIRONMENT OF THE FIRM

The Economic Environment

Economic forces affect organizations in every part of their activities as they are a major influence on the various exchange processes. For example, the price of resources, both physical and human, the nature of demand and the perceptions and confidence of businessmen are all influenced by the economic environment. More specifically, a firm has to diagnose the relationship between itself and key economic variables such as:

- Inflation and the effect on costs and prices.
- Economic policy towards the cost of money and foreign exchange rates.
- Taxation, both direct on profits and indirect on employees and goods sold.
- The stage of the trade cycle and the effect on corporate performance.
- The economic mood of the country affecting investment and risk taking.

While all firms are affected by the economic state of the world and the economic policies of government, they will not all be affected in the same manner or to the same degree. Thus, the economic environment presents both threats and opportunities. For example, a period of recession may provide a company with a reason to produce lower price goods or to move overseas. Inflationary pressures on raw material costs may force a firm to seek cheaper imports or improved manufacturing methods. Higher disposable income may provide opportunities for new segments in the marketplace.

An understanding of the nature and dynamic of the economy and its effects upon a company is a key element in strategic planning. Often the planning process begins with a view of key economic indicators such as Gross Domestic Product (GDP) and inflation. For the manager, the problems are: what to look at, where to get it and how reliable are the data. There is a plethora of economic data available, published by the government, banks, specialist agencies, newspaper and magazines. All companies are affected by movements in macroeconomic variables but the extent of the sensitivity is learned through experience. As an example, sources of key economic indicators affecting primary demand are shown below.

United Kingdom National Accounts (The CSO Blue Book) (annual)	National GDP Sector GDP Total consumer expenditure and by commodity

British Business Magazine (weekly)	Producer prices, import penetration, exports, International comparisons
Family Expenditure Survey (annual)	Income and expenditure by households
Employment Gazette (monthly)	Employment, retail price index
Key Population and Vital Statistics (annual)	UK population and growth rates National and regional data
Bank of England Quarterly Bulletin (annual abstract)	Exchange rates International comparisons Longer runs of data on most economic variables

For many companies what is published is useful, particularly as a basis for forecasting, but it is historical data often published long after the event. For planning purposes, companies need a view of what will happen to the economy. For some companies, this means reading in the financial press the latest forecasts of, say, the Treasury model or the London Business School model of the UK economy. For others, there is a need to build their own models, particularly sector models, part of the rationale for model-building being the potential source of competitive advantage by having better and more comprehensive views of the economic environment affecting the company and its industry. More particularly, models show the relationships between variables, which for planning purposes is perhaps as useful as the results.

The Social Environment

Generally, the pace of change in the social environment which affects such factors as population size and structure and social values and expectations is slow but inexorable. Some social change is rapid, for example fashions and fads, but others take years, for example women moving into higher-paid occupations. The firm is affected not only in terms of the acceptability of its product offerings but also by such factors as attitudes to work, work practices and expectation of life-style. Social change as it affects a firm is often a complex of a number of seemingly differing phenomena. For example, the desire for one-stop shopping relies upon changes in work patterns and subsequent attitudes to leisure activities at the weekend, together with the acceptance of mass advertising by companies. Similarly, the change in the age structure of the population has created opportunities and threats for makers of baby products and suppliers of products and services aimed at the retired. The effects of social change are not confined to producers of consumer goods and services. The current debate on energy supply is much affected by society's attitudes to nuclear energy.

The Technological Environment

The pace of technological change in some industries has now become so rapid that product and process life-cycles have become much shorter. This is particularly true in the new-technology-based industries of electronic engineering, robotics and computing. While some industries may feel somewhat immune from such changes, technological developments in related industries can have a large effect. For example, changes in the technology of materials in the packaging industry have had a serious effect on the canning industry.

Technological developments potentially offer to firms the ability to purchase in greater quantity, with enhanced quality, and supplant labour with capital. Indeed, such is the impact of technology in some industries that the economic rationale of the industry is changed for all time, as in the use of robotics in mass car production.

The Political Environment

Government at both national and local level can affect companies not only on a day-to-day basis through laws, policies and its authority, but also at a strategic level by creating opportunities and threats. Specifically, such threats and opportunities arise because the government

- can determine the structure of an industry through monopoly and restrictive trade practices legislation;
- is a large supplier of fiscal and trade benefits through regional development programmes and industrial regeneration policies;
- is a large customer through defence contracts, civil works, education, health, etc.;
- can protect industries from overseas competition through competition legislation; and
- can affect the mood of enterprise by privatization or nationalization.

All firms are affected by the political environment but some owe their existence to government by being defence contractors, eductional equipment suppliers, hospital suppliers, etc. Such firms in a sense exist at the whim of government policy, which changes, often radically, after each election.

The Factor Market

The factor market comprises those imports of raw materials, labour and capital which are endemic to business. The relationship between a firm and its suppliers is discussed in more detail in chapter 6, but for the purposes of environmental analysis there are two aspects which are important in analysing the factor market. First, an important aspect of factor inputs is their availability. Difficulties in sourcing materials can lead firms to integrate backwards, thus internalizing their material supplies market. The availability of labour can pose severe problems for industry: hence some companies are forced into creating education programmes for new employees. Secondly, the price of factor inputs is important and often closely allied with availability. Price fluctuations make financial planning most difficult and may lead to serious attempts to substitute materials or suppliers. Some companies are sensitive to factor prices; for example, up to 80 per cent of turnover may be represented by raw material costs. Whatever the nature of the factor input, price fluctuation can have a serious effect on competitiveness.

The Product Market

The competitive environment is of such importance that it is considered in detail in the next chapter.

5.3 STRATEGIC POSTURE

The key managerial task is to ensure that the relationship between the firm and its environment is one by which the firm can attain its objectives. One of the major causes of corporate decline is that created by a mismatch between the firm and its environment. Thus, there is a strategic imperative not only to understand the nature of the environment and its dynamic but also to be aware of those environmental variables to which the firm is most sensitive. This is not an easy task in that there is no simple technique which will establish such a relationship; it is rather a matter of experience or organizational learning. However, due to cost constraints, few firms can monitor everything in their environment and thus there is a need to focus on the most sensitive environmental variables. The dangers of a strategic mismatch are obvious and can arise from any part of the environment via such factors as technological obsolescence, the gradual disappearance of a market segment served due to economic or social change, changes in legislation, raw material shortage and competition. Thus there is a need to take a forward view of the environment.

5.4 ENVIRONMENTAL FORECASTING

In many respects, taking a current view of the environment, although rewarding, misses the essence of strategy in that it is about the future, and thus a forward view is more important to strategic decision-making. How to forecast and the techniques to use depend upon the nature of the company. Single-product companies serving single-market segments will have a less complicated task than, say, multi-product, multidivisional multi-market firms. Further, the larger the firm, the more resources it may be able to devote to forecasting and increasing the sophistication of the techniques employed. Generally, most companies begin the process via informal, often verbal, methods. These would include talking to key people in the environment and to business analysts, reading the business press and 'talking to the City'. Those methods are fairly simple and cheap but they fall short of defining a relationship between the dynamics of the environment and the success of the firm. If a firm wishes to establish these relationships in a more scientific manner, then a number of techniques of varying degrees of sophistication are available. At the most simple level, single variable extrapolation is perhaps the most common. As with many forecasting techniques, it assumes the past is a guide to the future, and in the case of a product life-cycle it must be remembered that the firm's actions can alter its shape. For many companies who can isolate a key environmental variable, this may be rewarding. If a company's sales are closely correlated to a single environmental variable such as personal disposable income, then forecasts can be made simply on the basis of linear regression analysis. For many companies, however, a single environmental variable is insufficient, and thus multiple regression techniques may have to be utilized. At this stage of sophistication, further techniques such as factor analysis and input–output modelling are possible and useful. As was mentioned above, many of the techniques rely on the assumption that the past is a guide to the future; while this may be true for many relationships, any change in the relationship renders the method less useful and strategically dangerous. Techniques have been developed to attempt to forecast without relying heavily on past data. In essence, the techniques are subjective in nature but their use can be significant, particularly where there is little past data or the forecast horizon is well into the future. Such methods would fall into the category of expert opinion, which may be structured (as in the case of delphi techniques) or unstructured (as in the case of scenario generation). Delphi is particularly useful in the field of technological forecasting where the opinion of researchers in the field may be sought about the likelihood of a technological change.

Scenarios are useful in answering 'what if' questions without the use of simulation models. Thus a firm could postulate differing future environments with the use of expert opinion, and then look at the likely future impact on the firm in terms of when strategic decisions would have to made to react to such environments. Scenario generation has been particularly successful in taking very long-term views of the environment, particularly in the field of technology.

In essence, there are two approaches to scenario building. One method is to postulate the future on the basis of change which the organization cannot affect (unconditional) and the other is to take a view of the future when the company itself contemplates changes in its strategy (conditional). Thus, for example, a company could look at scenarios if it envisaged change in major aspects of, say, its own product-market strategy. This is rather akin to the notion of the company creating its own environment as a result of its own decisions. In practice, companies often have to develop multiple scenarios based on different assumptions and covering different aspects of the environment. Thus, for example, major oil companies develop political risk scenarios, environmental ones, worldwide economic/ energy ones, all of which provide views of the future which affect current decision-making, particularly with regard to the generation of contingencies as part of the planning process.

A common question in the field of strategic environmental forecasting is how far ahead one should look. Much depends upon the reaction time to environmental change, which in turn may be influenced by the production technology the firm is using. For example, it takes considerably longer to create capacity for steel manufacture than, say, to produce a piece of new software. If a company wishes to respond strategically to a perceived future change in the environment, then decisions about such a change in strategy may have to be taken some time in advance. This can be shown by gap analysis techniques as shown in figure 5.4.

The line F_1 is a desired strategic parameter, e.g. profitability market share etc., whereas F_2 is what will happen if there is no change in strategy, so by Year 2 a gap is beginning to emerge. The major problem is thus how

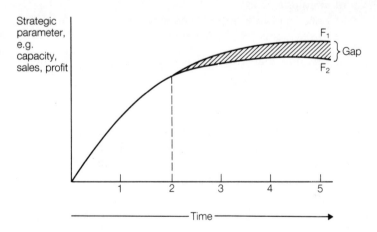

FIGURE 5.4   Gap analysis

long it takes for current decisions to begin to fill the gap. Clearly, in the example of an integrated steel plant, two years is too short a time period, for the capacity may not be on line in two years if it is to be built from a greenfield site. Thus, forecasts will have to have a time horizon which can encompass design, construction and commissioning of plant. The other strategic options would be to buy the plant from someone else or to subcontract.

Forecasting for strategic decision-making probably does not have the precision requirements of other forms of forecasting, particularly as the time horizon lengthens, but unlike short-term forecasting the outcome of such forecasts can result in larger resource commitments as part of a strategy. Thus there is an inevitable trade-off between risk and accuracy, which is partly accomplished by firms having experience in monitoring the environment continually as part of the strategy creation process.

5.5   MANAGEMENT SUMMARY AND CHECKLIST

Outlined below are some examples of the kind of issues that would need to be examined in the various environments.

Economic Environment

What effect are the following economic variables likely to have on the operation of the business?

- rate of economic growth
- level of unemployment
- level of prices and rate of price changes
- balance of payments (BOP) position.

What effect are the following policies and issues likely to have on the business?

- monetary policy
- fiscal policy
- specific BOP regulators such as tariffs, quotas, exchange rate changes, etc.
- specific prices and/or incomes legislation
- measures to reduce unemployment.

In addition, further information may be necessary if expansion is to take place in an economy in which the company has no previous experience:

- size of Gross National Product (GNP) and GNP per head
- income distribution.

Social Environment

What is the likely impact on the business of changes taking place with respect to the following social issues?

- health and welfare
- recreational needs, e.g. sports, arts
- education
- living conditions – housing, amenities, pollution
- working conditions
- social changes – discrimination, equality, population trends.

Technological Environment

What impact are developments in the technological environment going to have on the business?

- transportation technology
- energy use and costs
- biological sciences
- materials sciences
- mechanization and robotization
- computerization.

Political Environment

What impact are developments in the political environment going to have on the business?

- Socioeconomic system: ownership, control, regulation and deregulation
- Competition policy: legislation on monopolies, restrictive practice and advertising
- Government: nationalized industries, employer, purchaser, and guardian of individual, local and national interests.

Factor Inputs

Labour markets and trade unions

- Is there a continuous supply of the necessary labour skills, both manual and technical?
- Are there problems with trade unions with respect to demarcation and working practices?

- Is the business unionized or becoming more unionized – what are the implications?

Materials and services

- Are there problems in obtaining supplies of raw materials? Problems with foreign sources of supply?
- Does the price fluctuate wildly?
- Is the industry becoming more vertically integrated, which would affect supply?

Capital and money markets

- Are there problems of raising money for the businesses we are in or into which we seek to enter?
- Where is the best country to raise capital?
- What is the likely future for interest rates?

Product markets

A detailed approach to analysing markets appears in chapter 6.

Customers

- Who are our customers and potential customers?
- How big are our customers?
- How important are our top ten customers to our business?

Competitors

- Who are our competitors and potential competitors?
- How big are our competitors and are they part of a large group?
- Is competition increasing from buyers or suppliers?

6 Understanding Industries and Markets

Introduction—Market, Industries and Competition–
Structure and Competition—The Learning Curve—
A Model for Competitive Analysis—Generic Competitive
Strategies—Competition and Growth—Buyer Behaviour—
Management Summary and Checklist

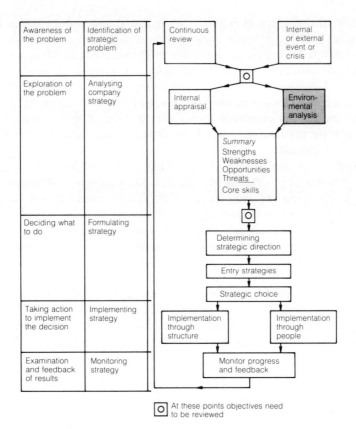

FIGURE 6.1   The strategic decision-making process

6.1   INTRODUCTION

Although forming part of environmental analysis, the competitive environment is singled out in this chapter for a number of reasons. First, it is seen by businessmen as the most important environment with which they have to deal.[1] Secondly, of all the external environments, the competitive environment is probably the one where firms spend the greatest amount of resources, chiefly in the area of marketing. Thirdly, it is perhaps the most proximate environment in that its effects on the organization are continuous and direct; thus organizations are dealing with it daily. Finally, it is composed of actors whose behaviour will normally be directed as a threat to an organization.

6.2   MARKETS, INDUSTRIES AND COMPETITION

For many, the distinction between an industry and a market has little importance. For the strategist, however, the distinction can be crucial. The essential difference is that an industry is an output concept, while a market is a demand concept. Normally, industries are defined by the Standard Industrial Classification whereby all firms supplying a particular product or service are grouped together. While for some forms of analysis this may be a useful statistic, it says little about competition; it merely states who supplies. Thus, for example, the output of Rolls Royce and Ford would be aggregated together.

From the strategist's point of view what is of most importance is the nature of competition, that is, the market. Markets can be described and defined by the nature of competition. Thus, if the strategy of one company has a marked effect on demand for the output of another, then it can be said that the two firms are in competition with each other. What therefore matters in defining market boundaries is the degree of substitutability between products. To return to the Rolls Royce/Ford example, it can clearly be seen that for most of the Ford product range there is probably no competition between the two companies, and thus they are not in the same market. A further aspect of the definition of a market is that the company can begin to realize that competition can arise from another industry – as, for example, when the chemical industry entered the textile industry with man-made fibres.

6.3   STRUCTURE AND COMPETITION

Economic theory provides a useful starting point from which the strategist can begin to analyse the consequences of market structure. A number of concepts are important in such analysis: namely, the number and size of competitive firms, the degree of substitutability of the product and the ease of entry into and exit from the market. Thus market structures can range from monopoly to perfect competition. Generally, the more perfect a market appears to be then the less power any one competitor has to influence price. However, markets can exhibit differing degrees of concentration. The degree of concentration is an important strategic concept, as increased concentration usually delivers market power into fewer hands; further, if concentration results in larger outputs for some companies, then (coupled with market power to set the pace of competition) such firms can gain cost advantages through economies of scale and the effects of the learning curve. Thus it would appear to follow that firms with large outputs and significant relative market shares have both revenue and cost advantages over smaller companies. Thus, for the smaller company the strategic problem becomes one of 'How do I compete?' For the large company the question, while the same, has a further strategic complication in that powerful competitors may well be able to match or better any strategy pursued by one of them to gain a competitive advantage. This latter phenomenon may well result in competition among the large few becoming rather orderly so as not to 'upset the boat'.

6.4   THE LEARNING CURVE

The learning curve, or experience curve, represents the relationship between costs and output. Unlike economies of scale, costs fall because the firm learns to produce more efficiently because of its accumulated experience. Typically, costs of manufacturing can fall by between 20 and 30 per cent each time output doubles. The effect is not automatic, as companies have to realize the potential for cost saving. Thus, a firm on an 80 per cent experience curve should expect a 20 per cent drop in costs each time output doubles. Cost savings arise out of better use of labour, materials and capital. A firm may consciously attempt to gain experience through research and investment.

6.5   A MODEL FOR COMPETITIVE ANALYSIS

So far it can be seen that there are a number of structural concepts which are important to the analysis of competition in a particular market. Essentially, what is of interest is the relationship between market structure and market behaviour. This has two major aspects. First, what does any one company have to do to compete successfully in a market; and, secondly, what can a company do in terms of strategy in order to obtain a strategic advantage? The first is bound up in the norms of market behaviour. These are such that in certain types of market there are things which all firms have to do in a particular manner. Examples are advertising in consumer goods industries, R&D in 'high-tech' markets, capacity planning in high-volume industries etc. The second aspect is more concerned with doing these things better than competitors to gain an advantage.

Thus a recognition of the relationship between structure and behaviour is an important input into the strategic analysis procedure. As has been stated by Porter, 'competition in an industry is rooted in its underlying economic structure and goes well beyond the behaviour of current competition.'[2] Porter's model provides a useful framework for analysis as shown in figure 6.2. An important feature of the Porter model is that, while the concepts are not new, they have been assembled into a total model which provides insight for the strategist. As can be seen from the model, the competitive environment includes not only the output market but also the input market. This is sensible in that input decisions from the factor market greatly affect a company's strategy.

Generally, the forces of competition drive an industry towards a profit level which is sufficient to keep firms in the industry. The strategic task, therefore, for any company is to deploy resources so that it can make profit levels in excess of what is normal, that is, that profit level which keeps it in production. As can be seen, therefore, a number of threats to the pursuit of profit are posed. First there is the threat of new entrants. The ability of firms to enter the market is determined by the nature of barriers to entry. Where they are low, entry is relatively easy and the consequence of such entry is that profitability is shared among most firms, thus reducing individual company profits. The erection and maintenance of high entry

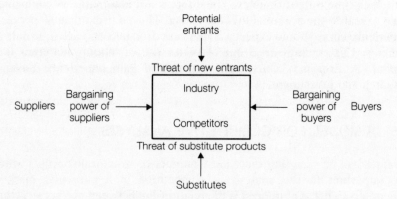

FIGURE 6.2   Forces driving industry competition
Source: M. E. Porter, *Competitive Strategy* (Free Press, Glencoe, 1980).
Reprinted with permission.

barriers may depend upon patent protection, output scale, learning curve effects, proprietary knowledge, tying up distributors etc. or merely on competitive excellence. It may even pay individual firms in the long run positively to create such barriers through pricing or promotion to keep new entrants out of the market.

The second major threat is from substitute products. Clearly this is most apparent in commodity markets where competing products are perfect substitutes. However, even in this situation a firm may be able to differentiate its product offering through non-product benefits such as service. A major strategic effort may therefore be devoted to product differentiation based either on non-product features or on the product itself. This should not be confused with market segmentation which, although it may have the same effect, is based on providing differing product offerings for different types of customer or buyer. Although potentially attractive, differentiation or segmentation has associated costs. The wider the product line the less the potential production and marketing economies of scale available. In addition, advertising is spread more thinly, and production runs may be smaller. Similarly, the dynamic of the market may be such that great effort has to be put into product innovation to keep a competitive lead.

Thirdly, buyers can exact pressure on a company. The more concentrated the buying market *vis à vis* the producer the more power it will have. For example, the grocery industry has concentrated greatly in the past ten years, giving it more power over producers. Supplying firms can become heavily dependent on one or two retailers which gives retailers great power in such aspects as price negotiation and product quality and quantity. However, switching source of supply can be expensive for buyers, and to some extent high switching costs give producers more power. The fourth element of the model (the bargaining power of suppliers) can be seen as the reverse of the bargaining power of buyers.

Overall the model is useful, for once the company has taken a view of the inputs, various strategic parameters emerge. Thus a company in a highly concentrated industry dealing with a basically undifferentiated product will have different strategic options than (say) a company in a highly fragmented industry producing and selling a heavily differentiated product. As with most models, its efficacy depends upon 'what if' questions to get sensible answers. An important 'what if' question relates to the value of growth in the market, which forms the next issue in this chapter.

6.6   GENERIC COMPETITIVE STRATEGIES

The ultimate objective of any firm is to gain a superior position over that of its rivals. This has many advantages, not the least of which is that the profits will not be eroded as easily by the forces governing the competitive process. The question, therefore, is how does a company gain and sustain a superior position or, more precisely, upon what types of generic strategy does a firm gain a competitive advantage?

Porter advances a number of answers to the question based upon four important concepts.[3] Does the firm seek to gain advantage by being low cost or through differentiation such that buyers will pay a premium based on their perceptions of the product? Further, does a company seek to serve a number of segments in the marketplace or focus on a few? This may be seen diagrammatically in figure 6.3. There is, of course, a fifth strategy where companies have not decided where the balance and thrust of their strategy lie and these companies may be termed 'stuck in the middle'.

	Low cost	Differential
Multi-segment	Cost Leadership	Differentiation
Fewer Single Segments	Low cost focus	Differentiation focus

FIGURE 6.3   Generic competitive strategies
Source: Adapted from M. E. Porter, *Competitive Strategy* (Free Press, Glencoe, 1980) with permission.

In summary, the differing strategies require differing market conditions as well as differing skills, for example cost leadership requires tight cost control and sets of customers who perceive the benefit of low costs translated into prices. Differentiation requires strong marketing and often R&D as well as distinctive requirements from people. Further, the product has to be perceived by customers as offering something unique to them for which they are prepared to pay a premium. The risks of both strategies are that market conditions change, rendering them obsolete or that they are imitated by others, eroding any competitive lead a company may have, particularly when the company cannot sustain its advantage.

The choice of a generic route to a sustainable competitive advantage by a company has an effect upon its profitability. Further, there is a relationship between profitability and market share. Figure 6.4 shows the relationship between absolute size of any competitive advantage and the number of means of achieving such an advantage.

Size of advantage

	Small	Large
Many	Fragmented	Specialization
Few	Stalemate	Volume

No. of approaches
to achieve advantage

FIGURE 6.4   The new BCG matrix
Source: Boston Consulting Group, 1982. Reprinted with permission.

6.7   COMPETITION AND GROWTH

A useful starting point in market analysis may be to take a view of the nature of growth in the total market or any segment under analysis. The concept of the product life-cycle is useful in this context, although its use as a strategic planning tool may be limited, as its shape may be altered by the action of the company and thus it becomes more of a self-fulfilling prophecy.

An important note of caution when using the concept of the product life-cycle is to distinguish between the product life-cycle for an individual product and the cycle for the market within which that product competes. Both are useful to strategic analysis, but here emphasis is placed on the market life-cycle where the strategic implications of each stage will be discussed (see figure 6.5).

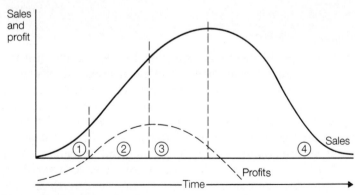

Four stages may be determined:
1 Introduction or Development   3 Maturity or Saturation
2 Growth   4 Decline

FIGURE 6.5   The product life-cycle

Introduction or Development

In this stage, market growth is slight and there will probably be little differentiated demand. However, from a firm's point of view a great deal of expense may have been incurred in R&D, and in product and process design. In addition, marketing costs will be high, due to market research, test marketing, promotion and setting up distribution channels. It is thus highly unlikely that profits are made in this stage. The major strategic decision will have been made before this stage begins, namely, to develop and launch the product. Any firm at this stage will have predicted or hoped for the next stage in the pre-launch analysis. Certainly product performance in the marketplace will have to be closely monitored, for if the market does not grow, major decisions will have to be made regarding withdrawal from the marketplace with the attendant costs and loss of goodwill.

Growth

This stage is characterized by rapid growth in sales and profits. Profits accrue due to the increase in output. Larger market share may result in price leverage and lower costs due to scale and experience effects. At this stage it is cheaper for firms to increase their market shares as the market grows. Further, some marginal firms may have been shaken out of the market. Product lines will have settled down to serve distinct segments and such standardization should lead to lower production costs.

Maturity or Saturation

This is perhaps the most common stage for all markets. It is in this stage that competition becomes most intense as firms strive to maintain market share. Thus marketing and finance become key functional areas within corporate strategy. Further, it is in this stage that market segments emerge in greater numbers. Attempts to grow market share at this stage are expensive as, given little market growth, aggressive strategies of gaining share from competitors are expensive and lead to retaliatory moves. Any growth at this stage will depend upon growth in such variables as GNP, population etc. and thus forecasting may be easier. As this stage is normally the longest lasting, the greatest profit will be made. Thus firms will not wish to incur large expenditure on R&D and product and process design of a fundamental nature. Rather, such expenditure will normally be directed to product modification and improvements in plant capacity and quality.

Decline

As the market growth rate declines it does not necessarily follow that firms should quit. It may be possible for a firm to stay in the market to gain a large share of a declining market but this strategy has a finite limit, that is 100 per cent of nothing. Above all, great financial care has to be exercised during this stage. It may be possible to strip cost out of the product in order to maintain profitability by cutting back on promotion or on volume, or by variety reduction. Similarly, the product could be 'niched' by production for a smaller subset of the market where a large market share can be obtained. The product could be taken to new overseas markets. Any end game strategy at this stage depends upon the rate of decline in the market and the consequent effect on revenue and the consequent decision on withdrawal. Many firms have pulled out too quickly when careful financial decisions would have maintained product profitability. A further aspect to the problems of this stage concerns the launch of new products which will replace existing ones. This is particularly important for such aspects as after-sales service, stocks, distribution and production.

6.8   BUYER BEHAVIOUR

A fundamental consideration in market analysis concerns itself with the nature of demand. It is perhaps too comforting to presume that buyers will buy. Increasingly, companies are interested in questions such as when, how, why and how often? An intimate knowledge of buyer behaviour is properly the preserve of the marketing function, but it has important consequences for corporate strategy. Any firm's product offering represents its views of the market and thus is a tangible message to the environment, including such aspects as image and status. Thus a company has to consider the strategic implications of market analysis.

Few, if any, markets are composed of buyers with homogeneous needs, and it is the differences between needs which create opportunities for market segmentation and subsequent product positioning strategies. Buyers' needs are a complex of demographic, social, economic and psychological variables. When sufficient buyers of a particular type constitute a viable subset of the market, firms can consider developing specific strategies for that segment. To be viable the segment must be profitable, identifiable and capable of being communicated with. Any shortfall within these criteria renders segmentation difficult.

Basically, a firm has three options. First, it can deem differences to be unimportant and follow a policy of mass marketing where the product is undifferentiated. Secondly, recognizing differing segments, it can produce differentiated products and strategies designed to suit the needs of each segment. Finally, it can choose to concentrate on one segment only. The choice depends upon capability and the risk/return trade-off. What is important is that the strategy of the company has been 'fine-tuned' to take account of differing segments.

A further dimension is the notion of product positioning. Again, this depends on a full knowledge of buyer behaviour in that firms have to think about those product features which allow them to be successfully placed in a market. For example, suppose a company wishes to market a new hand tool and it knows that there are two important purchase considerations: price and maintenance. Thus, a product space map of the market would appear as in figure 6.6.

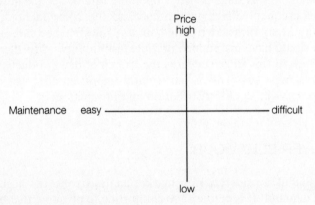

FIGURE 6.6   Product space map

What is of strategic importance is where to place the product. Consideration will include the position of competing companies' products and of the company's own existing products, the perceptions of buyers to a different or similar position, the profit potential and the nature of the company's image.

As can be seen in both the examples of segmentation and positioning, an understanding of buyer behaviour is important to strategy. Many firms have simply 'run out' of a market by failing to understand this important aspect of market analysis.

6.9   MANAGEMENT SUMMARY AND CHECKLIST

Market and competitive analysis is a useful and integral part of strategic analysis involving the whole of the organization. A thorough understanding of the market is essential to corporate strategy. In a sense, a firm's product or service offering represents how well a market is understood by a company and as such is 'voted on' immediately by customers. This attempt to understand the structure and dynamic of a market should form part of the strategic process by asking key questions as summarized below:

1 What is the degree of concentration in the market?
   To calculate concentration it is necessary to know:
   (a) the number of competitors;
   (b) the market share of each competitor.
2 What size is each competitor? Are they part of a large group of companies?
3 How closely substitutable are competitors' products?
4 Are there any entry barriers?
5 Are there any exit barriers?
6 Where are our company and our competitors on the learning curve?
7 Is entry to the market likely to come from our suppliers?
   This would be forward vertical integration for the supplier.
8 Is entry to the market likely to come from our customers?
   This would be backward vertical integration for the customer.
9 Are companies currently not making the product or supplying the service likely to enter the market?
10 Are technological or other changes likely to generate a substitute product?
11 Where is the product on the product life-cycle?
12 What changes are taking place in the competitive environment and what are the implications of these changes?

NOTES

1 W. F. Glueck and L. P. Jauch, *Business Policy and Strategic Management* (4th edn, McGraw-Hill, New York, 1984), p. 134, for examples of surveys of the views of strategists concerning the importance of different external environments.
2 M. E. Porter, *Competitive Strategy* (Free Press, Glencoe, 1980).
3 Ibid.

7 Internal Appraisal

Introduction—Strengths and Weaknesses—Analysis—
Objectives—Strategy—Structure—Finance—Marketing—
Production—Research and Development—Personnel—
Systems and Procedures—Matching the Internal and
External Environments—Management Summary
and Checklist

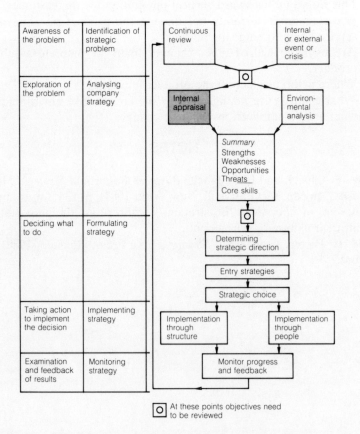

FIGURE 7.1 The strategic decision-making process

7.1   INTRODUCTION

The major task of strategic analysis is concerned with an organization taking a view of itself in order to assess its current strategic position. Put more simply, the organization is attempting to ascertain, through analysis, its strengths and weaknesses. Such an analysis is by no means simple, for it involves the firm taking a dispassionate view of itself, and given the nature of most organizations, objectivity is often difficult to achieve. Further, it must be remembered that any corporate strength can only be defined in terms of strategic importance – it is no good being good at something unless it contributes to the well-being of the organization. However, where a firm has a strength which is crucially important to its effectiveness, then it can assume the ownership of a highly prized asset and the firm can be said to have a distinctive competence in that area. A list of possible distinctive competences is shown in figure 7.2. The analysis has one further use in

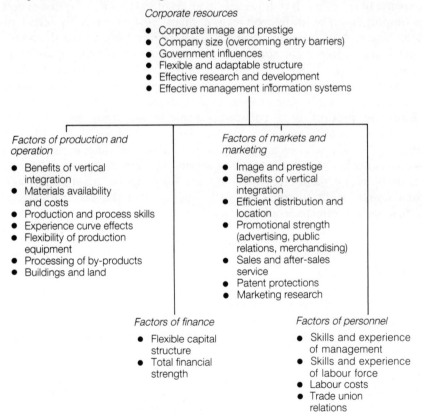

Corporate resources

- Corporate image and prestige
- Company size (overcoming entry barriers)
- Government influences
- Flexible and adaptable structure
- Effective research and development
- Effective management information systems

Factors of production and operation

- Benefits of vertical integration
- Materials availability and costs
- Production and process skills
- Experience curve effects
- Flexibility of production equipment
- Processing of by-products
- Buildings and land

Factors of markets and marketing

- Image and prestige
- Benefits of vertical integration
- Efficient distribution and location
- Promotional strength (advertising, public relations, merchandising)
- Sales and after-sales service
- Patent protections
- Marketing research

Factors of finance

- Flexible capital structure
- Total financial strength

Factors of personnel

- Skills and experience of management
- Skills and experience of labour force
- Labour costs
- Trade union relations

FIGURE 7.2   Core skills and key resources
Source: G. A. Luffman and R. Reed. *The Strategy and Performance of British Industry 1970–80* (Macmillan, London, 1984). Reprinted with permission.

that, once a firm has taken a view of its internal strengths and weaknesses, not only does it have the results of a strategic audit but such data give the firm ideas for future strategy by matching its strengths to future environmental opportunities. Further, the company can begin to do something about its weaknesses.

7.2   STRENGTHS AND WEAKNESSES

The proposition assumed above that a firm should play to its strengths while improving upon its weaknesses presupposes that a firm knows its current position. How then does a firm know what it does well and what it does badly? Any corporate competence is composed of two parts: those things which a firm can do efficiently and those which it can do effectively. They are not mutually exclusive, nor should a firm attempt one at the expense of the other. It is, however, in terms of strategy that the distinction is important. The distinction can perhaps best be seen in terms of advertising. Any campaign can be efficient in terms of cost per thousand, opportunities to see etc., but its effectiveness depends upon creativity in design, copy etc. In some instances effectiveness can compensate for lack of efficiency and vice versa. For example, a small producer who cannot gain the same production economies as a larger competitor can market a distinctive product to a particular segment, and thus his marketing effectiveness compensates as long as he can maintain that marketing strategy. Conversely, in a price-sensitive market, production efficiencies which result in lower prices may compensate for poor marketing. Thus any analysts asking themselves what are the firm's corporate strengths and weaknesses ought to carry out such analysis with the key variables of efficiency and effectiveness uppermost in their minds.

7.3   ANALYSIS

An important prerequisite in corporate appraisal is what to look at. In one sense the answer is everything, but a useful checklist is composed of the key features of the organization, normally defined by function. Such a list is shown below:

- objectives
- strategy
- structure
- finance
- marketing

- production
- research and development
- personnel
- system and procedures

Some of the above can assume crucial importance as a result of the nature of the business, and others appear to be important because they deal with the whole organization. Examples of the latter case are objectives, strategy and finance. Thus they are afforded separate treatment elsewhere in this book (see chapter 4 for objectives, part III for strategy and chapter 8 for finance). However, as all of the ingredients of strategic internal appraisal are examined at the same time, those which are treated in greater depth elsewhere are included in this chapter for reasons of completeness.

7.4 OBJECTIVES

The impact of objectives in internal strategic appraisal is twofold. First, the results of internal appraisal will provide a significant input into objective setting. Thus the firm will create objectives based upon its views of its distinctive competences or strengths. Secondly, objectives will provide guidelines against which to measure the performance of many internal factors within a company. Thus it should be possible to isolate those key internal factors which enhance or detract from a firm's ability to achieve its stated objectives.

As can be seen, objectives are reference points for corporate performance and as such they need to be clearly identifiable. To be of most use, objectives should be measurable, achievable, realistic and communicable. Vague statements about growth and profitability suffer from imprecision, which when performance needs to be assessed, renders meaningful analysis difficult.

The need for reasonable objectives means that commonly they are set in terms of economic performance. This in turn entails some statement about profitability. While it may be argued that profit is itself a means to an end, it is a sufficiently well-accepted measure of performance towards which all firms are striving that it can be recognized as a primary objective. A major problem with objectives arises in organizations which are not for profit, such as museums, art galleries, charities etc. Here the problem is to determine a useful parameter against which to measure organizational performance.

A common problem is to distinguish between strategy and objectives. Often statements from senior managers about their company contain a mixture of both. For example, statements such as increase turnover, grow overseas, divest, improve product quality, spend more on research, may well be objectives for parts of the organization but generally they are means to some greater objective such as company profitability.

From a strategic viewpoint, objectives will translate themselves into lower-order objectives for functions or departments within the organization as is shown in figures 7.3 and 2.2. Thus there has to be an internal consistency between corporate and operational objectives. For example, if a firm has decided that an objective of a rate of return on capital employed of 20 per cent is desirable, then this ratio can be decomposed into its component parts, or (in the example) if an average margin of 10 per cent is further desired

$$20\% = 10\% \times 2$$

which means that given the two objectives of return on capital employed (ROCE) and margin, a capital turnover ratio of 2 is required. To be internally consistent, the organization has to be capable of such a performance. Thus to achieve consistency, objectives may well be the result of an iterative process which will achieve such consistency.

7.5 STRATEGY

Strategy is a word which has been most widely used in the military sphere. However, recently the word has been used extensively in business and, as in the military context, may be defined as 'the means of achieving a given objective'. A strategy is concerned with integrating company activities and allocating scarce resources, so that the present objective can be met. In the process of planning a strategy, it is important to appreciate that decisions are not taken in a vacuum, but that any action taken by the business firm is likely to be met by a reaction from those affected: competitors, customers, labour force or suppliers. It is critical, therefore, that the effects of such reactions should be evaluated before taking decisions. Such an evaluation may lead to the abandonment of the project, to a contingency plan, or to making plans which minimize the effects of possible reactions.

The conceptual view of strategy and the relationship of strategy and objectives have been outlined above. It remains, therefore, to discuss the meaning of strategy in operational terms.

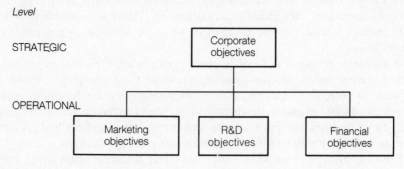

FIGURE 7.3   Relationship between corporate and operational objectives

Strategy is concerned with: (a) products and technology; (b) markets and customers. A company can only stay in business by satisfying customers. Thus, for given financial objectives, a company must decide what markets and customers it is going to supply, what products will be made to satisfy those customers, and with which technological process it will manufacture the products.

It must be remembered that often a firm's strategic options are severely limited. It is rare for a company to market products to a set of customers in a totally different manner from its competitors. Thus, often a company is not just interested in the effectiveness of a given strategy; it is also concerned about its efficiency. As strategy is a most important aspect of business policy, it is discussed in greater detail in part III.

7.6 STRUCTURE

Any strategy has to be deployed through an organization, and thus an important aspect of strategic appraisal concerns itself with the appropriateness of organizational design.

Figure 7.4 illustrates a simplified form of a functional organization where the individual functional managers of the firm are responsible to the chief executive. The ultimate responsibility for the direction and control of the company will lie with the board of directors, and the functional managers may or may not be members of this board. (If they are they will be directors of the company.)

Figure 7.5 illustrates a simplified form of a divisional structure in which the main feature is that each division or subunit of the company operates in

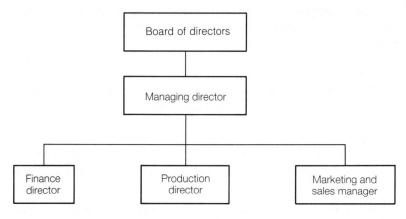

FIGURE 7.4   Functional organization structure

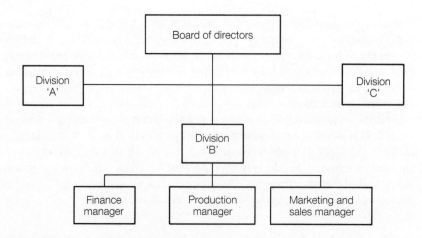

FIGURE 7.5   Divisional organization structure

semi-autonomous fashion, separated from the other units. This type of organization would more easily fit a diversified company with interests in, say, pottery manufacture in one division and textile fabrics in another. There may often be little relationship between these divisions and hence little purpose in having, for example, a marketing director responsible for overall marketing activity. In the divisionalized structure we could expect differing performances from the divisions, and consequently they may justify the allocation of different targets by the board according to their particular product and environment. In general, the board will have overall financial control and will seek to reinvest where it feels it can make the best return on investments. Thus we may see profits flowing out of one division to be invested in another, with appropriate decisions being made at board rather than divisional level, although production and marketing decisions can be taken at divisional level by the individual managers involved.

The multidivisional diversified company is already one of the most important forms of organization, not least because it allows marketing and production autonomy at divisional level while retaining financial control at the centre. Nevertheless, it does not follow that all organizations should be shaped this way. For the small company and the company engaged in a limited product/market area, the functional organization can still be effective.

However, following strategy formulation, we do need to address ourselves to the question of whether the existing organization structure is appropriate to the implementation and monitoring of the strategic plan. We need, therefore, to ask the following questions before deciding:

1   What is going on at the moment in the company with respect to product flows? For instance, is the company vertically (or horizontally) in-

tegrated in any way? Are these internal transactions (for example, product flows between units may require counterbalancing resource flows) appropriate in relation to the markets dealth with?

2   Does the present organizational structure facilitate these flows around and out of the company?

3   If the company has been subdivided in any way (functional or divisional), are these subdivisions congruent with the measures of performance and rewards desired by the company?

A simple illustration covering the latter point would be the case of a marketing manager whose performance (and subsequent rewards) is judged by sales returns, distribution in stockists and so on. If, however, he was in conflict with the production manager whose performance was measured in part by minimizing of stock-holding costs (resulting in lost orders and possible customers), then the 'organization' would not be congruent with respect to performance measures. Thus, either the organization should be changed or the performance measures allocated to the participants varied in order to achieve improvements.

Matrix Organizations

Matrix structures are arrived at in some organizations normally because there are two operations which require significant amounts of management. Thus, for example, line management might constitute one area of management and staff management another. Similarly, product or market management may be an important area, and functional management is also important (see, for example, figure 7.6). A further example can be seen in R&D management (figure 7.7). Its use as an organizational structure is independent of the scale of operations, and it possesses some distinct advantages. It balances competing managerial priorities and thus can improve decision-making. Any one manager in the matrix has to coordinate his activities, thus improving contact within the organization. However, the drawbacks of such a structure are that individual managers may have difficulties in reconciling competing claims on their efforts with

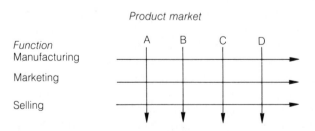

FIGURE 7.6   Product market management matrix

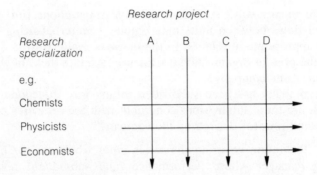

FIGURE 7.7   R&D management matrix

consequent demotivation. Responsibility is often hard to pinpoint and subsequent protracted discussion may slow down decision-making.

7.7   FINANCE

As a corporate function, finance has many aspects which are concerned with strategy, as shown below:

- the acquisition of funds;
- the use of such funds, including project appraisal;
- the provision of information to outsiders, including the preparation of final accounts;
- the provision of internal information – the management accounting function;
- the provision of information from outside the company.

Thus, although not a line function, it is possible to take a view of its strengths and weaknesses like any other department of a business. Essentially, its function consists of two parts: first, those activities concerned with the funding of the company; and, secondly, those concerned with monitoring the use of those funds. This latter function will spread across the whole organization and will be chiefly concerned with monitoring and control systems.

Funding and investment decisions are fundamental to corporate strategy. The amount and mixture of long- and short-term debt can have serious implications for corporate performance. For example, the mixture of capital has implications in terms of future repayments and dividends. Thus a firm which borrows loan capital will have to be certain that the returns from such investment can cover at least future interest payments, and the price of the loans will be important. In this respect loan capital may be available from many sources at differing prices; thus part of the finance function responsibility is knowledge of the market for funds.

Capital investment decisions are closely linked both to strategy and to funding decisions. The appraisal techniques and models available to screen such decisions fall in part under the remit of the finance function. Thus part of the efficacy of the finance function can be gauged by its knowledge of capital investment appraisal techniques and their limitations.

The role of the finance function as a data source and information provider is important to the control of strategy. An important part of any strategy is to create and schedule control systems which will monitor its performance. Thus decisions regarding the frequency and amount of information should be taken as part of corporate strategy formulation. The quality of such information is the responsibility of the finance function. Financial information is often of two types, that which constantly flows to monitor the performance of strategy, and that which is needed less frequently but often in greater depth, for example in financial appraisal of a potential takeover victim, new product proposal, new market, divestment etc. Imperfections in the speed of preparation and quality of such information can result in poor strategic decision-making.

The analysis of company performance is often found to be a problem for non-accountant students and analysts, and as such is considered in detail in chapter 8.

7.8   MARKETING

In a corporate context, marketing has two important functions. First, any strategic analysis could investigate the market orientation of the total enterprise. In this sense marketing is more than the function of the marketing department as it involves every function, realizing that customer satisfaction is a total responsibility. Secondly, marketing is a function within a company primarily concerned with demand management. Marketing at this functional level is responsible for positioning the company's product offering in the marketplace. This involves researching the market and focusing the market response into a particular market segment. The other major task, to assemble the company's marketing strategy, is often referred to as the marketing mix. The marketing mix is that combination of product policy, promotional policy, pricing policy and distribution which is assembled to meet the needs of the market segment and which will give the company a competitive advantage.

The amount of resource devoted to marketing will depend upon the nature of the market. For example, firms in highly competitive markets which have many buyers with diverse needs (such as fast-moving consumer goods) will devote more resources to marketing than, say, a company with few customers with special needs and limited competition. Whatever the amount devoted to marketing, the function is important in that it is the link between the firm and its customers and its strategy has a high visibility in the environment.

Competition provides a useful basis for companies in assessing the strengths and weaknesses of the marketing function. Comparisons can be made with other companies for it is rare to find competing companies conducting their marketing in such differing ways as to render comparison difficult. External comparison is not the sole method of assessment for, as with other functions, the relationship of marketing with other functions is important. For example, what demand does marketing place on production in terms of product quality and quantity? How good is market planning in terms of giving reliable forecasts for other functions in the organization?

7.9 PRODUCTION

Production is normally defined as that process which transforms tangible raw materials into saleable products or services, with the result that many of the techniques and concepts of production can be applied to the production of services. Further, the methods of strategic appraisal are common to both products and services.

Any strategic appraisal of the production process will concern itself with the efficiency and effectiveness of plant, equipment and production labour, which in turn necessitates an analysis of manufacturing costs, capacity, location and those systems inherent in production such as maintenance, quality control, stock control and production scheduling.

A significant strategic advantage is provided by the ability of a company to lower production costs for a given quality compared with competitors and to react quickly to changes in demand through good production scheduling or by having flexible plant. Such abilities depend upon the competence of production staff to purchase the right plant and machinery and to appreciate the importance of cost consciousness. The impact and nature of production costs has an important strategic aspect. For example, consider two companies with differing cost structures, where Company A has a low ratio of fixed to total costs, Company B has a high ratio of fixed to total costs. These are shown in figure 7.8.

The analysis is simplified by having a common sales curve. As can be seen, Company B has a higher break-even point, but once past break-even its profits rise at a faster rate than those of Company A whose break-even is lower. Thus Company B is volume sensitive in that any fall in volume will have a greater impact on B than on A. The consequence for production is that heavy investment in plant will increase fixed costs, particularly where

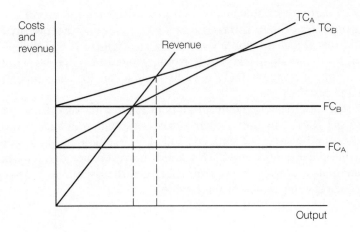

FIGURE 7.8   Product cost structures
FC, fixed costs; TC, total costs.

such investment replaces labour, and thus volumes need to be high to compensate. This phenomenon is particularly prevalent in service industries such as banks and insurance companies who have a high ratio of fixed to variable costs. However, if a company can gain a high sales volume then the additional plant can lead to economies of scale or cost saving through the experience curve effect. Similarly, large outputs often mean that the firm can afford better technology and specialist personnel.

7.10   RESEARCH AND DEVELOPMENT

Research and development includes a wide range of activities from fundamental research to product improvement. Generally, expenditure in this area is designed to promote new product development, product improvement and manufacturing process improvement.

The decision to devote resources to R&D is in itself a strategic one, based on a corporate desire to improve products and processes internally rather than buying the research needed or to be an innovator and leader rather than a follower and imitator. The risks associated with R&D expenditure stem from its ability to deliver new products or cost savings in production. The risks associated with not spending or with under-spending are a loss of technological expertise, lack of new product and process ideas, and an over-reliance on new ideas being commercially available.

A key strategic decision is how much to spend on R&D and, within the broad spectrum afforded by the area, where to spend scarce resources.

Although certain technologically based industries tend to spend a significant proportion of their turnovers on R&D, it does not necessarily follow that all firms in such an industry will adopt an offensive R &D policy; some may prefer to imitate quickly, thus avoiding high research costs. However, in the imitating company there must be some technological competence to assess the research.

A further approach to the uncertainty problem with R&D expenditure is to give the R&D function a clear market orientation in such a way that projects will be assessed and controlled in relation to their potential marketing payoff. This approach should, however, not detract from the fundamental strategic analysis of R&D which essentially assesses the technological competence of the function.

7.11   PERSONNEL

The major role of the personnel function in terms of corporate strategy is to ensure that the quality of personnel is consistent with the jobs defined. Thus personnel or human resource management – for the task is more than the function of the personnel department – involves the recruitment, development and appraisal of personnel, together with the creation of reward and welfare systems.

When well managed, a company will have high morale, good relationships among different levels, high job satisfaction resulting in low labour turnover and absenteeism. The ability to measure some of these factors is somewhat limited, but there are obvious signals when things go wrong such as measuring absenteeism, labour turnover and industrial disputes.

In addition to the above factors, any appraisal of the human assets should investigate teamwork: how well do certain groups, such as the board, senior managers, project teams, work as a team? This is particularly important for certain key strategic tasks such as policy creation, new product development, corporate planning and strategic appraisal.

Increasingly, as markets become more hostile and firms are looking for product and process innovations to secure strategic advantage, many firms are attempting to release an entrepreneurial spirit in the organization. This is difficult in a more bureaucratic structure, but many companies are attempting to create a corporate culture which fosters entrepreneurship with all the associated attitudes to risk taking. Clearly, the ability to foster such attitudes to innovation depends upon the culture of the company which is the responsibility of senior management. Culture change is neither easy nor quick, but its impact is pervasive, affecting many aspects of human relations and management in an organization.

7.12 SYSTEMS AND PROCEDURES

Often firms neglect the various systems in a company as part of the strategic appraisal, but in one sense the whole exercise is part of a corporate planning system. There are others such as information systems, communication systems, budget systems, which are company wide and not necessarily dependent on any one function. Their efficiency and effectiveness can have an important effect upon the viability of the organization and are compounded, often, with size. The bigger the firm, the more complex such systems become. The advent of new technology has improved the ability of companies to handle the necessary data, but the systems have to be designed and be capable of adaptation with changes in corporate strategy. Two major aspects are of importance; first, does the firm have a particular system and, secondly, how good is it? As has been mentioned, one would expect that as firms grow, then certain types of system would be incorporated or, if in existence, made more sophisticated (see table 7.1).

Thus it would be unusual for a large firm not to have a corporate planning system. How good it is depends ultimately upon user needs, in that the systems must fulfil the needs of decision-makers. Thus the question of what information goes to whom and what is done about it needs to be asked. Further, such systems have their own objectives which should not be incongruent with those of the organization. For example, a financial system designed to prevent fraud may involve a bureaucracy which slows down decision-making; thus a firm has to make the necessary trade-off between the elimination of fraud and more rapid and responsive decision-making.

Often such systems are difficult to adapt without penalty, but they are an important part of the company and thus need to be appraised regularly.

7.13 MATCHING THE INTERNAL AND EXTERNAL ENVIRONMENTS

The preceding chapters have shown what has to be taken into account when analysing an organization and its environment. In a sense the analysis is akin to a strategic audit but, unlike a financial audit, it not only concentrates on what is but also on what might be. The task is to assemble the analysis into a meaningful shape in order to plan future strategies. Emphasis has been placed on the determination of corporate strengths and weaknesses and environmental threats and opportunities. These may be shown diagrammatically in figure 7.9.

Any strategy should build on strengths towards opportunities while avoiding threats and correcting weaknesses. This is the important link

TABLE 7.1 Stage process audit criteria

Criteria	Stage I: Initiation	Stage II: Contagion	Stage III: Control	Stage IV: Integration
Data processing (DP) organization				
Objective	Get first application on the computer	Broaden use of computer technology	Gain control of DP activities	Integrate DP into business
Staffing emphasis	Technical computer experts	User-orientated system analysis and programmers	Middle management	Balance of technical and management specializations
Structure	Embedded in low-functional area	Growth and multiple DP units created	Consolidation of DP activities into central organizational unit	Layering and 'fitting' DP organization structure
Reporting level	To functional manager	To higher level functional manager	To senior management officer	VP level reporting to corporate top management
User awareness				
Senior management	Clerical staff reduction syndrome	Broader applications in operational areas	Crisis of expenditure growth	Acceptance as a major business function
			Panic about penetration in business operations	Involvement in providing direction

User attitude	'Hands-off' Anxiety over implications	Superficially enthusiastic Insufficient involvement in applications design	Frustration from suddenly being held accountable for DP expenditures	Acceptance of accountability Involvement in application, budgeting, design, maintenance
Communication with DP	Informal Lack of understanding	Oversell and unrealistic objectives and schedules Schism develops	Formal lines of communication Formal commitments Cumbersome	Acceptance and informed communication Application development partnership
Training	General orientation on 'what is a computer'	Little user interest	Increase in user interest to accountability	User seeks out training on application development and control
Planning and control				
Objective	Hold spending at initial commitment	Facilitate wider functional uses of computer	Formalize control and contain DP expenditures	Tailor planning and control to DP activities
Planning	Orientated towards computer implementation	Orientated towards application development	Orientated towards gaining central control	Established formal planning activity
Management control	Focus on computer operations budget	Lax to facilitate applications development activity growth	Proliferation of formal controls	Balanced formal and informal controls

Criteria	Stage I: Initiation	Stage II: Contagion	Stage III: Control	Stage IV: Integration
Project management	DP manager responsibility	Programmer's responsibility	Formalized system DP department responsibility	Formalized system tailored to project DP and user/management joint responsibility
Project approval and priority setting	DP manager responsibility	Multifunctional managers First in, first out	Steering committee	Steering committee Formal plan influence
DP standards	Low awareness of importance	Inattention	Importance recognized Activity aggressively implemented	Established standards activity Published policy manuals
Objective	Prove value of computer technology in organization	Apply computer technology to multifunctional areas	Moratorium on new applications Consolidate and gain control of existing application	Exploit opportunities for integrative systems Cost-effective application of advanced technology
Application justification	Cost savings	Informal user/manager approval	Hard cost savings Short-term payout	Benefit/cost analysis Senior management approval

Source: Reprinted by permission of the *Harvard Business Review*. A table from 'Controlling the Costs of Data Services' by Richard L. Nolan (July/August 1977). Copyright © 1977 by the President and Fellows of Harvard College (all rights reserved).

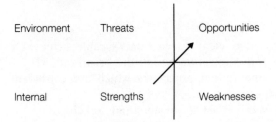

	Environment	Threats		Opportunities
	Internal	Strengths		Weaknesses

FIGURE 7.9   Summary of internal and external analysis

between analysis and strategy selection and, although it may appear simple, its efficiency depends upon the quality of analysis. The listing of strengths and weaknesses by an organization, while often not an easy task, often results in a picture which is not totally revealing. The danger is that what may be listed turns out to be a collection of symptoms rather than causes for an organization's material health. For example, declining sales is not a problem but a symptom of perhaps something rather more deep seated, which strengths and weaknesses analysis fails to reveal. The key question is why has an organization ended up with a particular set of strengths and weaknesses? Such a simple question affords deeper analysis looking for causality. This often results in a much shorter list of core skills or, in competitive terms, answers the question: what are our differential strategic advantages?

This further process is important, for once an organization understands its competitive differential advantages or core skills then such knowledge is powerful in guiding its future actions. Further, it allows the company to compare itself with critical success factors for the industry. All companies have to answer the question: how do we compete? In many industries there are critical factors which all competitive companies have to be competent at to be credible, but superior performance in one or more of them places that organization in a superior position with consequent effects upon profitability.

7.14   MANAGEMENT SUMMARY AND CHECKLIST

For the business analyst or the student with the case study, a checklist will be useful. The checklist can be made more effective by weighting the degree of relative strength or weakness by use of a semantic or numerical scale which allows statistical manipulation or profiling. The checklist below is illustrative rather than exhaustive and refers to the relevant sections in the chapter.

Objectives

- Are the objectives clear, explicit, measurable, achievable, realistic and capable of communication within the organization?
- Are there operational objectives which are consistent with overall strategic objectives?
- Will the objectives satisfy owners and stakeholders?

Strategy

- Is the strategy consistent with objectives and the resource capabilities of the organization?
- Does it build directly on strengths?
- Does the strategy realize synergy within the company?
- Is the strategy appropriate for the company's environment?

Structure

- Is the organizational structure consistent with the declared strategy?

Finance

- Has the company sufficient financial resources to fund its strategy?
- Is the mix of funding flexible?
- How low is the cost of capital?
- Can the company raise new capital?
- How effective is financial planning and control?

Marketing

- How efficient and effective are the component parts of the mix?
- How strong (in terms of market share) is the company in the markets served?
- How effective is product development?
- How good is the company at market research and at identifying trends and gaps in the market?
- What is the relationship between turnover and profits?
- What is the relationship between profits and the customer base?

Technology

- How does the company compare in terms of production cost?
- How does the company compare in terms of production quality?
- How up to date is the production technology?
- How effective are the production systems for maintenance, quality control, production scheduling, stock control?

- How easily can new products be assimilated into production?
- How near to full capacity utilization is the company?
- How flexible is the plant?
- Are we producing in the right location?
- Is purchasing taking advantage of bulk discounts?
- Is there a major sourcing problem with scarce raw materials?

Research and development

- How technologically competent are the staff?
- How good are the laboratories and equipment?
- How market orientated is R&D?
- How much is spent on R&D?

Personnel

- Is the recruitment policy developing the number and quality of people required to implement strategy?
- Is the training policy developing the necessary new skills and improving existing competence?
- Is the management development programme providing the quality of management necessary to implement the corporate strategy?

Systems and procedures

- Are the systems and procedures providing the means by which strategy can be implemented?

From the foregoing it can be seen that strategic internal analysis is a large task. For many companies it is an annual process; thus it has its own learning curve. Further, it must be remembered that many internal features of a company do not require much lengthy analysis; they are often very obvious. Such features as competitive strength, cost structure and profitability are often obvious. Similarly, it is possible to purchase details of competitors' performance as well as sector analysis which gives a useful set of data with which to compare oneself. However, the task remains that of the company. Evidence suggests that such an analysis often explodes many myths within organizations, forcing, as it does, management to take as objective a view as possible. The analysis is, however, of little value unless it is placed against the nature of the current and future environment facing the company, and this is discussed in part III.

8 Financial Appraisal

Introduction—The Nature of Financial Statements—The
Balance Sheet—The Trading, Profit and Loss
Account—Ratio Analysis—Adjusting for Inflation–Share
Valuation and Strategy—Cash Flow—Management
Summary and Checklist

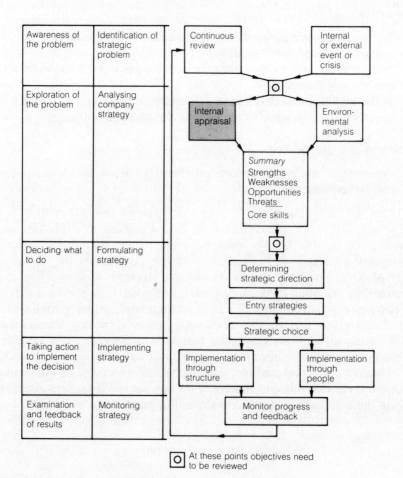

At these points objectives need
to be reviewed

FIGURE 8.1 The strategic decision-making process

8.1 INTRODUCTION

The relationship between corporate appraisal and financial analysis is most important. The analysis of an organization's performance through its reported financial statements is fundamental to an understanding of business policy. Such analysis has two components:

1 It provides important evidence of total corporate effectiveness, particularly when measured against previous performance or that of similar companies.
2 The efficiency and effectiveness of the finance function can be assessed in terms of the acquisition and management of financial resources.

Such analysis is not confined to business policy, as many bodies external to the firm are interested in performance, for example, banks, stockmarkets, trade unions, competitors, suppliers and investment analysts.

Specifically, such analysis is concerned with assessing the financial health of a company and thus is designed to provide answers to key strategic questions. In addition, the analyst is interested in the degree of risk associated with the company as well as its returns to owners.

8.2 THE NATURE OF FINANCIAL STATEMENTS

Before proceeding to an explanation of the use of financial analysis in business policy, it is perhaps appropriate to explore the nature of the major financial statements used in such analysis. Generally, the most appropriate statements are the profit and loss account and the balance sheet. While other statements may be important, these two often provide sufficient data for analysis of corporate performance. To understand their creation and use, it is pertinent to look at the way in which a business is financed.

8.3 THE BALANCE SHEET

The balance sheet of a company is a device for showing the economic state of a company in a standard form. It is *a snapshot in time* of the state of the system described in figure 8.2. Essentially, it shows the *sources* of finance used by a company and the *assets* which have been acquired with these funds.

By itself the balance sheet does not, as is often widely believed, explain how successfully the company has fared over the year – this is the role of the profit and loss account – but, rather, gives a 'true and fair view' of the

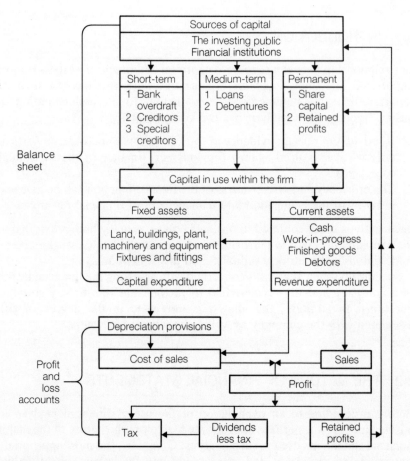

FIGURE 8.2　Sources of finance
Source: G. Ray, J. Smith, 'Handy Developments Ltd', in *Text and Cases in Management Accounting* (Gower). Reprinted with permission.

company's financial position at *the moment in time* when the balance sheet statement is prepared (see tables 8.1 and 8.2).

8.4　THE TRADING, PROFIT AND LOSS ACCOUNT

The purpose of a trading, profit and loss account (see table 8.3) is twofold; first, it is to measure the size of the profit or loss for the trading period and, secondly, it is to indicate the factors that have caused profits to rise or fall. The actual period covered by the account is determined by the management, and in practice it may be compiled monthly, quarterly or half-yearly

TABLE 8.1   Balance sheet 1

Sources of finance	Assets
1 *Share capital and reserves* Ordinary share capital Preference share capital Reserves – retained profit	4 *Fixed assets* Land and buildings Plant and machinery Vehicles Fixtures and fittings
2 *Long-term liabilities* Debentures Loans	5 *Current assets* Stocks Debtors Cash
3 *Current liabilities* Bank overdraft Creditors Tax payable Dividends proposed	

These days the balance sheet is more usually shown in a vertical form:

TABLE 8.2   Balance sheet 2

Share capital and reserves _____

Long-term liabilities _____

Long-term capital employed £ _____

Fixed assets _____

Current assets _____

less Current liabilities _____

Current assets –
Current liabilites = Net current assets _____ _____

Net assets employed £

for management information purposes although for taxation and reporting reasons, it is produced at least every 12 months.

The trading account calculates the gross profit or mark up which shows how much has been earned (gross) to cover the business expenses and leave an acceptable profit.

TABLE 8.3   Pro forma: trading and profit and loss account for Company X

Year ended 31.12.19XX

	£	£
Sales		
Deduct cost of sales	———	
Gross profit		
Deduct Selling expenses		
Administrative expenses		
Financial expenses		
	———	———
Net profits for the year (before tax)		
Deduct		
Corporation tax		———
Net profit after tax		
Deduct		
Dividends		———
Profit retained for the year		———

Gross profit = Sales revenue − Cost of sales

The profit and loss account charges selling, establishment and financial expenses against the gross profit, to arrive at net profit.

Net profit before tax = Gross profit − Indirect expenses

The profit and loss appropriation account 'appropriates' the net profit between the corporation tax assessed, the dividends proposed for distribution to the shareholders, and the amount to be retained in the business and added to reserves.

Retained earnings = Net profit before tax − Tax − Dividends

8.5   RATIO ANALYSIS

Four major areas may be defined as being of particular importance to strategic appraisal:

		Accountancy terms
1	Is the business profitable?	Profitability
2	Is the trading position satisfactory?	Trading
3	Is the business solvent?	Liquidity
4	Is the business properly funded and using those funds wisely?	Gearing

These questions can give rise to a host of relevant ratios derived from the financial statements. Which to use depends upon the problems to be answered, but generally there are some standard ratios to be calculated for each of the areas. Which ratio to use and the particular formulation is not critical as long as the same version is used each time to ensure consistency.

Profitability

Three ratios are of interest. First, how well have the owners of the company fared? Secondly, how productive have the company's investments in assets been with respect to profit and, thirdly, how productive have the net assets been?

The relationship between the three ratios is shown in figure 8.3. For the purpose of consistency, PBIT is used throughout and is defined as sales

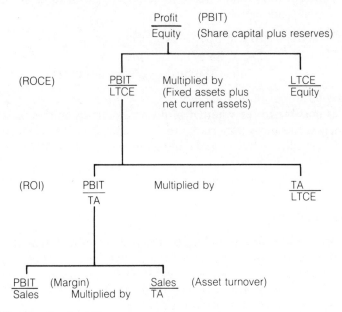

FIGURE 8.3 Profitability ratios
PBIT, profit before interest and taxation; ROCE, return on long-term capital employed; LTCE, long-term capital employed; ROI, return on total assets; TA, total assets.

minus (cost of sales plus indirect costs) or, alternatively, net profit before interest and taxation. The actual meaning of the ratios is discussed below.

Returns to owners:

$$\frac{PBIT}{Equity}$$

shows how well the legal owners of the company are faring. If analysis requires the amount of PBIT which could be distributed to owners, then PBIT becomes net earnings, i.e. profit after deducting tax and interest payments (PAIT).

Return on capital employed:

$$\frac{PBIT}{LTCE}$$

shows the total profits which the invested capital has produced.

Return on investment:

$$\frac{PBIT}{TA}$$

shows the profits created by the firm's investment in both fixed and current assets.

The rate of return on total assets can be broken down to show how profitability is made up:

$$ROI = \frac{PBIT}{TA} = \underset{(Margins)}{\frac{PBIT}{Sales}} \times \underset{(Asset\ turnover)}{\frac{Sales}{TA}}$$

Thus it is possible to see whether profit arises due to margin or turnover and which is the most important. In some industries like food retailing margins are traditionally low and thus turnover becomes a vital producer of profits.

Trading Position

When examining a firm's trading position, analysis is designed to show what sort of returns are being made for a given sales level or investment in assets. Put another way, analysis should show the productivity of sales and assets and the relationships between them. Standard ratios which can be calculated in this area of analysis include:

$$\frac{Sales}{Capital\ employed}$$

i.e. the number of times capital is represented in sales. Generally, if there have been no great distortions in either of the figures, the higher the ratio the better.

PBIT	i.e. operating profit to sales. Margin viewed over time
Sales	shows one of the principal means of earning profit. Clearly, the higher the better, but any fall in margin would lead the analyst further to enquire why. Is margin being given up to maintain market share? Are costs out of control? etc.

Sales	i.e. how productive are the assets? Provided there are
Fixed assets	no distortions in either figure, the higher the ratio, the more productive the assets.

Sales	A similar ratio to the above in that it shows the
Working capital	productivity of net current assets.

Sales	How many times in a year is stock being turned over?
Stock	

Liquidity Position

Like many ratios, liquidity ratios have to be viewed in terms of the nature of the business. Many industries typically run on low liquidity margins. Further, a great deal depends upon when the final accounts are presented, and firms with seasonal earnings will exhibit quite differing degrees of liquidity throughout a year.

Current ratio	Current assets	essentially poses the question
	Current liabilities	'Can the business pay its way in the near future, that is, if the stock is sold and debtors realized?'

Liquidity ratio	Liquid assets (current assets less stock)	
'Acid test'	Current liabilities	'Can the business pay its way immediately?'

Technically, if the liquidity ratio is less than 1:1 the business is insolvent, but great care should be taken in making such statements as liquidity standards vary from industry to industry.

Gearing

The two major sources of long-term funding for any business are loan capital and issued share capital. How a firm finances itself is a strategic decision, the results of which can have serious implications for the health of a company. The relationship between the two sources of finance is termed 'Gearing' and is expressed as:

$$\frac{\text{Loan capital}}{\text{Capital employed (loans + issued capital)}}$$

	Company X	Company Y
No. of £1 issued shares	1000	500
Long-term debt (10% interest)	–	500
Capital employed	1000	1000

Thus Company Y is 50% geared.

If the profit and loss accounts for both companies are examined, then the picture presented in table 8.4 emerges.

TABLE 8.4   The effect of gearing

| | Year 1 | | Year 2 | |
	Company X £	Company Y £	Company X £	Company Y £
Sales	1000	1000	1000	1000
Operating profit	200	200	50	50
Interest payable	–	50	–	50
Profit remaining	200	150	50	–
Tax (50%)	100	75	25	–
Profit after interest				
and taxation	100	75	25	–
Earnings per share	10p	15p	2.5p	–

The effect of gearing is that profit which could be distributed or ploughed back disappears to debt holders through interest payments and thus the ability of a firm to pay its interest becomes important. The impact of debt charges can be assessed by calculating a firm's interest cover expressed as:

$$\frac{\text{Profit before tax and interest}}{\text{Interest}}$$

Secondly, however, the earnings per share in the geared company are better than those in the ungeared company in Year 1 because the geared company pays less tax. In Year 2 the effect of gearing is to wipe out profit. Thus any firm has to recognize the long-term consequences of gearing in terms of the ability to pay the interest and the effect on profitability.

Earlier it was shown that when arriving at profitability ratios the effect of gearing could be seen. For example, returns to owners will be affected by gearing. Similarly, the composition of debt is important. As has been shown, firms can finance themselves by a mixture of long- and short-term debts; thus the relationship shown in figure 8.2.

$\dfrac{\text{LTCE}}{\text{Equity}}$ shows the proportion of long-term capital employed which is financed from equity,

whereas $\dfrac{\text{TA}}{\text{LTCE}}$ shows the proportion of total assets financed from long-term capital, the difference between these being short-term finance such as overdrafts, creditors and unpaid tax. While not all of this short-term finance is free (for example, overdrafts carry an interest charge), many of them are free forms of short-term capital which can be used to finance profit-yielding assets. This mode of finance is heavily used in food retailing, for example, where stock which is purchased on (say) two-month credit terms is sold in (say) two weeks, generating profits for the benefit of shareholders without their having to finance these stocks.

The constraints on the extent to which a company can grow can be determined by its ability to raise finance. Finance is raised from only two general sources: in the form of loans from banks, for example, and from the shareholders in the form of equity. All financing is at heart a variation of one of these. For example, retained earnings are a form of equity in that they belong to the shareholders and are not distributed to them. In that sense they are equity. Similarly, deferred tax owing to the government is a 'loan' from the government due to be paid at a future date just like a bank loan.

The key to raising finance from either of these two general sources of equity or loans is the past performance of the company. Bankers are happy to lend to successful companies and shareholders are happy to subscribe to rights issues or to retention of earnings when this is reflected in a rising share price. Hence there will be a maximum sustainable growth rate which will be determined by the return of equity in the firm. The maximum sustainable growth rate is then given by:

$$\text{Growth rate} = \frac{\text{Debt}}{\text{Equity}} \; (r-i)p + rp$$

where

r = return on capital employed
i = rate of interest
p = proportion of earnings retained

A simplified example is as follows:

	£mn
Sales	840
Profit before interest and tax	84
Interest paid	12
Profit before tax	76
Tax paid	26
Profit after tax	50
Dividends paid	25
Retained earnings	25
Debt	126
Equity	200

$$\text{Return on capital employed} = \frac{84}{326} = 0.257$$

$$\% \text{ Earnings retained} = \frac{25}{50} = 0.5$$

$$\text{Rate of interest} = \frac{12}{126}$$

$$G = \frac{126}{200}\left(0.257 - \frac{12}{126}\right)\frac{25}{50} + 0.257\,(0.5)$$

$$= 0.18$$

The company therefore has a maximum sustainable growth rate capability of 18 per cent for the next year without recourse to further financing. If the company desired or planned for a higher growth rate than 18 per cent then it would need to take action on the component parts of the equation.

$\dfrac{\text{Debt}}{\text{Equity}}$ is the financing strategy of the firm and it could alter these proportions.

% Earnings retained is the dividend policy.

Return on capital employed is a function of its strategy, marketing and production policies.

The rate of interest is beyond the control of the company, although its credit rating will be affected by the factors above.

Debtors and Cash Flow

The ability of a company to collect the revenue is an important aspect of financial management and may be expressed as

$$\frac{\text{Debtors}}{\text{Sales}} \times 365, \text{ i.e. the number of days taken to collect debts.}$$

If the period is lengthening, this may indicate poor credit control or possibly the fact that the company is giving extended credit to gain sales. As with many ratios, much may depend upon the normal terms of trade in that industry.

In attempting a view of the financial health of a company it must be appreciated that there is often a relationship between the various ratios examined. The relationships between the ratios are shown in figure 8.4.

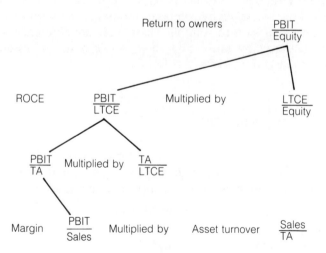

FIGURE 8.4   Pyramid of accounting ratios (the du Pont model adapted)

While some of the ratios may be difficult to calculate from the data presented in final accounts, the information will be available within the company, thus allowing the internal analyst the opportunity to see the relationships between the ratios.

Comparison

Any calculation of appropriate ratios for one year really does not tell the analyst a great deal. To provide a better basis of analysis, a comparative view should be taken, either with previous years or with similar organizations. However, to attempt analysis through time creates a difficulty due to the impact of inflation. Any financial appraisal should adjust for inflation in order to create a viable basis of comparison. How to adjust is relatively straightforward as is shown below in the section 'Adjusting for inflation'.

Several indices of inflation are available, perhaps the most useful being the RPI index of retail prices. This is published monthly in the *Employment Gazette* by the Department of Trade and Industry. However, for some industries this may be inappropriate, in which case *Price Indices for Current Cost Accounting* published by HMSO in the Business Monitor series may be utilized. This shows current indices for a variety of goods and services.

Comparative analysis with other companies can be difficult, as no two firms are exactly alike. However, it is possible to gather data via annual accounts to make comparisons, or, alternatively, data are commercially available from Inter-Firm Comparisons, Extel and Datastream. Much of this information is now accessible by computer terminal. The purpose of such a cross-sectional analysis is to point up where there are differences in performance as measured by ratios and then to begin the necessary investigations into these differences.

8.6   ADJUSTING FOR INFLATION

If sales and profits for a company are considered for two years (1970 and 1980) it can be seen that there has been an *actual* increase in both figures. However, if inflation is considered, a different picture emerges.

	Sales (£m)	Profit (£m)
1970	1000	80
1980	4000	160

The rate of inflation over the period can be taken into consideration by looking at the index of inflation figures (see above for source) for these years (1970 = 73.1, 1980 = 263.7), that is, £73.10p in 1970 would buy the same amount of goods as £263.70p in 1980. Thus, to make a meaningful comparison

$$1970 \text{ £s must be multiplied by } \frac{263.7}{73.1} = 3.61$$

or

$$1980 \text{ £s must be multiplied by } \frac{73.1}{263.7} = 0.277$$

If the figures are adjusted to 1980 £s, the 1980 figures remain as they are and the 1970 figures are multiplied by 3.61.

	Sales (£m)	Profit (£m)
1970 figures at 1980 prices	1000 × 3.61 = 3610	80 × 3.61 = 289
1980 figures at 1980 prices	4000	160

(Figures are rounded)

Thus, what looked like a fourfold increase in sales (£1000 in 1970, £4000 in 1980) is in real terms only [(4000 − 3610/3610) × 100 = 10.8%] increase and a doubling of profits (£80 in 1970, £160 in 1980) is in real terms [(160 − 289/289) × 100 = −44.6%], a 44.6% fall in profit.

8.7   SHARE VALUATION AND STRATEGY

As was mentioned at the beginning of the chapter, the performance of a company is a matter of interest to many parties. Thus the performance of a company as reflected in its share price is a visible commentary by the Stock Exchange. The ability of a firm to raise finance will be influenced by its share price. Further, certain key strategic events such as takeovers are heavily influenced by the Stock Exchange's view of the company. A key ratio in this area is the price/earnings ratio expressed as

$$\frac{\text{Share price}}{\text{Earnings per share}}$$

As can be seen, this will alter daily depending on the company's share price. Of itself, the price/earnings (p/e) ratio is not a particularly useful piece of information, except that it shows the market's assessment of the company. Generally, a firm with a high p/e ratio is indicative of the fact that the market expects more from the company.

The p/e ratio indicates how many years it would take to get back the purchase price at the current rate of earnings, assuming all earnings were paid out. This assumes zero growth in earnings. However, in the case of a takeover, the p/e ratio assumes a more important role. Supposing Company A is bidding for Company B and the following information is available:

	Company A	Company B
Issued shares (000s)	1000	500
Earnings last year (£000)	100	50
then Earnings per share (EPS) (in pence)	10	10
Price of shares (in pence)	100	100
p/e ratio	10	10

The market value of Company B is £$\frac{1}{2}$m, namely price of shares (£1) multiplied by number of shares (500,000); thus Company A in a share offer will have to offer Company B shareholders either £500,000 cash or 500,000 of its own shares, i.e.

$$\frac{\text{value of Company}}{\text{share price}} \quad \text{or} \quad \frac{£500,000}{100p}.$$

If, however, the share price of A is 200p with a p/e ratio of 20, then only half the number of its own shares would have to be offered, i.e.

$$\frac{£500,000 \quad \text{(B)}}{200p \quad \text{(A)}} = 250,000.$$

The obvious attraction of having to offer only half the number of shares, by having a p/e which is higher than the 'stock market average', places a premium on boosting and maintaining a high share price.

While the role of the p/e in takeovers is important, it is not the only factor to be considered in such strategies. For a fuller list of the principles employed, see chapter 13.

8.8   CASH FLOW

Cash flow is as important to a company as its profitability. This is because cash represents the 'life blood' of the company, allowing it to continue trading and also because lack of internal funding may necessitate the company having to raise money from outside, with the consequent effects on performance of interest repayment. Further, a profitable company can have a cash problem due to its success. For example, investment in new machinery may require new finance, increasing stocks may have to be financed from outside, and proposed takeovers may have a high liquidity content. Thus, for many companies, cash management is of equal importance to profitability.

Cash flows can present a number of problems to an organization. If demand is seasonal then cash flows will be seasonal, which means that often production takes place with little inflow of revenue; similarly, in the longer term, cyclical movements in demand may affect cash flow. From a strategic point of view these phenomena ought to be recognized and built into the forecasting process, so that cash shortfalls are seen in advance. The credit control system, while not increasing the size of the cash flow, should be designed to ensure that the speed of collection is such that it meets the firm's liquidity needs.

Although cash management in a strategic sense is concerned with future flows and amounts, a useful historical technique which may be used to assist in prediction is sources and uses of funds analysis. Basically, the analysis focuses on how the firm was financed and the uses which were made of such funds. Thus a source of funds would be any decrease in assets or an increase in a liability, while a use of funds would be represented by an increase in assets or a decrease in liabilities. This is shown in an expanded form below.

Sources

- increases in retained earnings
- increases in borrowings
- increases in issued capital
- reductions in cash
- reductions in stocks
- reductions in debtors
- sales of investments
- sales of equipment, plant, land and buildings.

Uses

- increases in assets
- increases in stocks
- increases in debtors
- reduction in creditors

Thus it is possible to see where the funds came from and where they went. Most published accounts now include such a statement, making it possible to analyse funds flows in an evaluative manner.

8.9 MANAGEMENT SUMMARY AND CHECKLIST

The remit of financial analysis should be sets of ratios and statements which allow the company to take a comparative view of its health. As such, the process and its outcome are an integral part of strategic appraisal.

A useful method of summarizing the financial analysis of a company is shown below.

Ratio or area of interest	Our company	Similar company or industrial sector	Comment
Profitability ROCE ROI EPS Growth			
Trading Sales/Capital employed PBIT/Sales Sales/FA Sales/WC Sales/Stock			
Liquidity Current ratio Acid test			
Gearing Loans/CE Dividend cover Debtor days			

PART III
Identifying Strategic Alternatives

9 Strategic Direction

Introduction—No Change Strategy—Vertical
Integration—Diversification—Strategy Based on Other
Criteria—Management Summary and Checklist

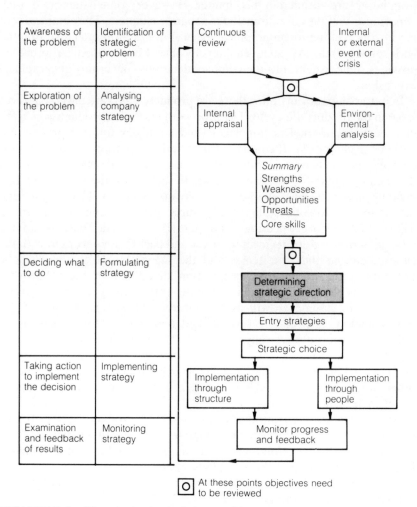

FIGURE 9.1   The strategic decision-making process

9.1   INTRODUCTION

The internal and external analysis has provided answers to the question 'Where is this company *now*?' The next stage is to determine what action the business needs to take to secure the desired long-term profitability goals. This is known as formulating strategy. There are several steps in the process of formulating strategy. Initially, it is important to decide on which products and markets offer the best means of achieving long-term company objectives. This is the concern of this chapter.

All the issues concerned in the question 'Where does this company go from here?' are outlined in this chapter. However, some issues are of such importance that they are discussed in separate chapters. The complexity of the factors relating to geographical expansion has promoted a substantial body of research. As such, chapter 10 'The Multinational Alternative' provides some insight into the complex decisions concerning geographical expansion.

In most company portfolios there are products which are past the growth stage in the product life-cycle. The process of managing products which are in a declining market is important, and strategies for this process are outlined in chapter 11. If companies fail to adopt appropriate strategies for declining products or for other reasons, they may experience a significant decline in profitability or even collapse. In such cases, there is often a fine dividing line between collapse and recovery. Chapter 12 evaluates the factors leading to collapse and the features of the situation which will or will not make recovery possible. Thus part III is concerned with identifying a range of possible strategic alternatives and part IV is concerned with the choice between these strategies and the means by which they will be executed, for instance through acquisition, divestment or internal growth.

There has been a tendency in corporate strategy texts either to focus on growth or to assume growth as an objective. However, in spite of this preoccupation, growth is rarely defined and reasons for growth as an objective are not always fully discussed. The implicit assumption is that growth means an increase in sales and profitability. However, the correlation between increases in sales and increases in profitability is negligible. In other words, increases in ROCE can be achieved by companies irrespective of their growth in sales.[1]

All companies have continually to review their product market offering as the environment in which they operate is constantly changing. Thus, alterations to their portfolio may result in growth, stability or a reduction in size as measured by sales or capital employed.

There are five basic directions that a company can explore when planning its future strategy:

- No change: manufacture or supply the same product or service to the same customers.
- Backward vertical integration: to manufacture or supply a product or service which is currently purchased from another company.
- Forward vertical integration: to manufacture or supply a product or service which is currently produced by a customer.
- Product extension: the development of the product offering from the existing product, through variants, to a completely new product offering.
- Market extension: the development of the markets served from the existing markets through entry to new segments, to sales to a completely different market.

The interaction of product and market extension leads to a variety of more specific directions, as can be seen in figure 9.2.

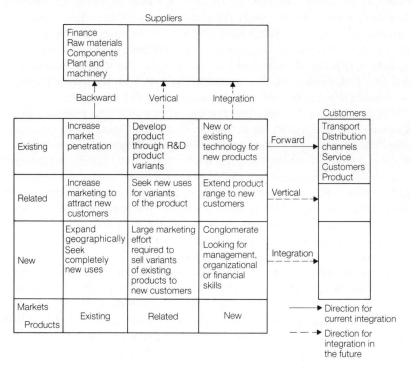

FIGURE 9.2   Directions for strategic development

9.2   NO CHANGE STRATEGY

There are several reasons why a company may pursue a strategy of no change in the short or medium term, although almost all companies will need to change in the longer run.

The first reason for a strategy of no change with respect to markets or products could be that maintaining or increasing market share at the early stages of the product life-cycle is the best use of available resources and that diversification will not enhance earnings. Secondly, that risks associated with diversification are not commensurate with the expected returns; and, thirdly, cash or other resources are not available.

9.3   VERTICAL INTEGRATION

The reasons why companies pursue strategies of vertical integration are complex. A basic classification of such reasons is defensive/offensive. Defensive reasons are to ensure the supply or quality of some essential raw material or component (backward integration) or to ensure an outlet for the product (forward integration). For instance, many holiday tour operators purchased aeroplanes in order to guarantee availability and quality of that part of the 'package' holiday. In the past, breweries purchased public houses to guarantee an outlet for their beer.

While defensive reasons for vertical integration are pursued by the company for self-protection purposes, there is little research to explain either the reasons for or the success of vertical integration. It is suggested that it is a high-risk strategy, in that a wholly vertically integrated company is more vulnerable than a horizontally diversified company as an interruption to one part of the process affects the total entity. There is some agreement that vertical integration does not take place at the early stages of the life-cycle and that, where it has done so, profitability has been depressed. Likewise, when the product is in decline vertical disintegration is a means of exiting from the industry gradually.

Most firms are a mixture of vertical and horizontal integration, with few of the sub-units being sole suppliers of any one other sub-unit within the firm. For instance, a carton-manufacturing company may sell cartons to several businesses within its own limited company and also sell to firms outside its own parent. More detailed explanation of linkages, their advantages and disadvantages can be found elsewhere.[2]

9.4   DIVERSIFICATION

There is no generally agreed definition of diversification as a strategy. In this section diversification will be used to describe extensions to the current portfolio on both the product and market dimensions. It is important to note that, while many of the frameworks (figure 9.2 for example) used to describe and analyse the product-market portfolio suggest one or two discrete categories, relatedness to existing products or markets is on a continuum from very closely related to no relationship at all.

An outline of the impact of alterations to the product-market portfolio is given in figure 9.2. Only existing products/existing markets would not be regarded as diversification, although existing products or markets to related products or markets would not constitute a significant change from current activity. It is supposed that the further a company moves from its existing product-market portfolio and the resultant core skills and key resources, the greater the possibility of failure. Unfortunately, the research evidence on diversification and performance is somewhat contradictory and, therefore, the expectation remains unsubstantiated.

It is important to note that *acquisition and diversification are not synonymous.* Acquisition may not lead to diversification (for instance, merging with a competitor) and diversification may be achieved through development within the company. Thus the reasons outlined below for prompting companies to seek products and markets outside their existing business relate to diversification and not acquisition, although some may be relevant to both. Acquisitions are discussed in chapter 13.

The first reason for pursuing a policy of diversification is that the current products and markets are incapable of meeting growth or profitability objectives. The emergence of a gap between objectives and expected results can be caused by the raising of objectives by an aggressive management or a shortfall in revenue and profit or a combination of the two. A closely associated reason is when a hitherto unforeseen opportunity occurs to increase profitability. Similarly, development through the firm's R&D department may lead to a diversification opportunity; there is the example of the Doulton pottery group diversifying into damp proofing of houses.

Some other motivations for diversification are:

- the advent of spare cash;
- the spreading of risk;
- the need to obtain some specific skills or resources which will significantly improve the performance of the existing business.

1   *Product line extension* is the addition to the portfolio of new products, some of which will be in a related technology and others in a completely

new technology. As many manufacturing companies often have significant distinctive technical knowledge and skills, they tend to stay in a given or closely related technology and expand into new or related markets. Less frequently, companies add a new product and a new technology to existing or related customers. This is usually effected through an acquisition; an example is the Quaker Oats acquisition of Fisher Price toys.

2   *Market extension* is the extension of the range of markets served by existing related or new products or services; for example, Allied Carpets move into curtains and furniture. Additionally, market extension can take the form of geographical expansion on a national basis, as in the case of Sainsbury's gradual move from the south of England through the midlands to the north. Also, the expansion can take place across national frontiers through exporting, licensing, joint ventures or complete manufacture and marketing facilities. It is at this point that the literature on international business becomes relevant, and international business issues are reviewed more fully in chapter 10. However, some primary motivations for such expansion can be seen from the results of a research study seeking to determine 'why companies expand overseas'.[3] The reasons most frequently given were defensive:

- to overcome tariff barriers
- to overcome transport costs and delays
- because of difficulties with agents and licences.

Aggressive strategies based on increasing profitability, lowering costs and so on were significantly less important than defensive strategies as a reason for expanding overseas. However, for many products, economies of scale and learning and experience-curve effects result in a domestic market of insufficient size to offer lowest long-term costs.

3   *New Product/New Market Extension – Conglomerate Diversification* is a very specific form of diversification. By definition, it is a move into a product-market area in which the company has no or few core skills either in marketing or technology. Possibly for this reason and the performance of several giant US conglomerates in the late 1960s, there is a suspicion, albeit not as strongly felt as in the 1970s, that they do not have a defensible corporate strategy. In terms of the efficient market hypothesis they ought to have low specific risk and consequently a low return. The low risk results from the portfolio effect of a large number of disparate businesses. However, some recent UK evidence[4] suggests that the returns are high and the risk low. The results, while in need of further corroborative evidence, would seem to indicate that the scepticism concerning conglomerate performance many need to be reviewed. As conglomerates have no marketing or technology links, the rationale

for their existence must lie in other functional areas of the business such as financial and organizational skills.

9.5 STRATEGY BASED ON OTHER CRITERIA

While most of the strategic changes made by companies are related to existing products or markets, some changes are based on other criteria, particularly financial. If a company is pursuing a corporate strategy based solely on financial criteria, it is likely that this will lead to conglomerate diversification; that is, it will be manufacturing a range of products and operating in a group of markets which have little or no relationsip with each other.

Companies which have a strong finance function are able to use these skills to improve company performance. This is usually achieved by means of takeovers which are the result of a process of continually scanning the business environment for victims that satisfy specific characteristics. Companies which have under-utilized financial resources are an obvious target. This could result from unused borrowing capacity or accumulated tax losses which could offset taxes on current profits under certain circumstances.

Another financially orientated criterion is the ability to make greater use of existing resources or, put another way, to increase profitability. Most conglomerates are examples of this skill. This may be achieved by eliminating low profitability activities or by the introduction of better financial or other management skills. The increased utilization of assets could come from the exploitation of some physical assets, such as property or mineral deposits on land owned by the company.

The wisdom of such widespread diversification which often results from financially orientated strategies has been questioned, particularly because of the activities of a few very large conglomerates in the late 1960s. As the focus of the corporate strategy is not products or markets, it is sometimes argued that there are no skills to ensure long-term profitability and as such financial strategies are opportunistic. Indeed, the increasing activity of corporate raiders and the advent of junk bonds has led to the situation in which a legal entity is brought into being with the sole purpose of purchasing and dismembering some giant company in the usually realized expectation that the parts are worth more separately than they are as a whole.

There is some evidence to suggest that the conglomerate strategy out-performs other strategies in times of depression but is outperformed by more focused strategies when trade is buoyant. Tube Investments is an example of a company which has moved away from a very diverse portfolio. In the early 1980s it might have been described as an engineering conglomerate but in recent years has become significantly more focused on three major products on a worldwide basis.

9.6   MANAGEMENT SUMMARY AND CHECKLIST

Businesses which are seeking to diversify need to approach the problem systematically. The first step is to determine in which direction this should be in terms of products or markets.

1   No change strategy

Companies at an early stage in the PLC can grow by developing their existing product to existing customers.

2   Vertical integration

This policy is pursued when a company wishes to control the sources of supply for some product or service which is used in manufacture of the current product range. Alternatively, the firm may wish to secure the outlet for a product.

3   Diversification

Diversification can take place on two dimensions, products or markets. Each dimension is on a scale from existing to new products or markets. If the product direction was both new products and new markets, this is referred to as conglomerate diversification.

4   Policy based on other criteria

If the company has differentiable skills outside marketing and technology, such as financial skills, it may choose to use these as a basis for diversification. This usually leads to the conglomerate form of diversification.

NOTES

1   G. A. Luffman and R. Reed, *Strategy and Performance in British Industry 1970–1980* (Macmillan, London, 1984).
2   M. E. Porter, *Competitive Strategy and Competitive Advantage* (Free Press, Glencoe, 1980 and 1985); J. Kreiken in W. Glueck, *Business Policy and Strategic Management* (3rd edn, McGraw-Hill, New York,

1980), pp. 256–63; K. R. Harrigan, *Strategies for Vertical Integration* (Lexington Books, Lexington, Mass., 1983).
3 M. Z. Brooke, and H. Lee, *The Strategy of Multinational Enterprise* (2nd edn, Pitman, London, 1978).
4 Luffman and Reed, *Strategy and Performance in British Industry 1970–1980*.

10 The Multinational Alternative

PETER J. BUCKLEY

10.1 INTRODUCTION

The simplest definition of a multinational firm is one which owns outputs of goods or services in more than one country. Such a firm adds value by producing in more than one national economy. The addition of value may involve increasing the quantity of goods, enhancing their quality or improving their distribution, both spatially and temporally. Such a firm therefore faces decisions on at least some elements of the 'marketing mix': price, product, promotion and distribution.

Multinational firms most usually control assets abroad through the medium of foreign direct investment. The act of foreign direct investment involves bringing income-generating assets under the control of a foreign corporation through purchase or through the creation of new assets. There are other methods of controlling foreign assets such as control through key inputs (normally technology), through management or other key workers (in, for instance, management contracts) or through joint ownership even if exercised by a minority stake. The element of control distinguishes direct foreign investment from portfolio foreign investment, which is usually carried out by individuals, not firms.

The control of assets and operations abroad, often on a vast scale, poses a number of problems in the economic management of the multinational firm.

10.2   THE INTERNATIONALIZATION OF THE FIRM

The Motives

Three main classes of motives for foreign direct investment can be identified:

- market orientated investments
- cost-reducing investment
- vertical foreign investment aimed at reducing the cost of raw materials or other key inputs.

Very rarely is a foreign investment decision taken for a sole overriding purpose. More often the motive is mixed, often even unclear.

There are a number of secondary or supporting motives which may come into the calculation. These can include:

- the investment climate of the host country (its tax regime, political stability, cultural closeness to the investor, provision of infrastructure);
- the firm's response to an external approach, perhaps by the host government, the firm's local agent or distributor, or from a customer, supplier or even a competitor;
- factors related to the source country, such as difficulties of supplying the market by other means, or as a response to a foreign investment by a competitor in the firm's home market.

The foreign investment decision is rarely taken for a single reason and rarely is it taken at a single moment of time. Rather it is the result of cumulative pressures and opportunities impinging on the firm. The process of foreign investment is akin to the building of a commitment in the firm.

The Process of Internationalization

The first foreign investment decision will be very different from subsequent investments. Initially, a national firm is likely to be very risk-averse as regards foreign involvement which is often seen as a leap into the unknown. Consequently, inexperienced foreign investors often require a strong stimulus even to begin to consider internationalization. Such stimuli can be internal to the firm, such as an executive with an interest in foreign expansion, or external, such as an opportunity presented by the firm's agent for instance. Such a stimulus will usually initiate a search for information, both general indicators on the host country and then on-the-spot investigation. Careful consideration is then made by key decision-makers before the decision to go ahead (or not) is made. In observing this management process, it may never be obvious at what point 'the investment decision' is taken. Far too frequently among inexperienced investors there is insufficient assessment and investigation, often leading to disastrous outcomes.[1] One particular error is the failure to specify clear performance targets for the new subsidiary.

The Route

It is unusual for a firm to go immediately to a foreign direct investment in a country without passing through a number of intermediate stages as illustrated by figure 10.1. From home activities only, such intermediate stages may be direct exporting, foreign agency representation and a foreign sales subsidiary before embarking on a full production subsidiary. It has been found that there is a direct positive correlation between the number of stages in the route and the ultimate success of the foreign subsidiary. This is because of the learning effects permitted at each stage of the longer route and because the intermediate stages allow the firm to withdraw before too much damage occurs. The full route (numbered 5 in figure 10.1)

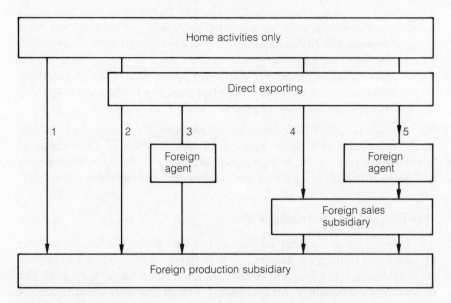

FIGURE 10.1   Routes to a foreign production subsidiary
Source: Reproduced from Peter J. Buckley, Gerald D. Newbould and Jane Thurwell, *Foreign Direct Investment by Smaller UK Firms* (2nd edn, Macmillan, London, 1988), p. 45, with permission.

allows for learning about the requirements of the foreign market in the exporting phase; the methods of doing business in the host country and how to deal with local people directly at the agency stage; the laws, taxes, how to control operations directly, selling, stockholding and promotion at the sales subsidiary stage; all in advance of having to cope with production problems abroad at the final stage. Foreign licensing or some other contractual arrangement may, of course, also be included as replacements or supplements for some of the above intermediate stages.

The Timing of the Move Abroad

The timing of a firm's move abroad is a very difficult management decision because it involves so much uncertainty and it is also very difficult to model adequately. The 'product cycle' approach to foreign direct investment suggests that the switch to foreign investment should occur according to the following cost-based formulation:

Investment abroad when $MPC_X + TC > ACP_A$

where MPC_X is marginal cost of production for export
    TC   is transport cost
    ACP_A is average cost of production abroad.[2]

The argument here is that marginal costings are appropriate for exports because domestic production would be undertaken anyway, while the foreign unit must bear the full average costs of production.

A fuller model of the switch to foreign investment is given by Buckley and Casson.[3] Essentially, two types of cost, fixed and variable, attach to the different forms of foreign market servicing: licensing, exporting and foreign direct investment. As the market grows, the variable cost declines and so the switch occurs from low fixed to low variable cost modes, typically from exporting to direct investment (see figure 10.2). This model is complicated when set-up costs are also included. Key variables in the timing of the move abroad are therefore the costs of servicing the foreign market, demand conditions in that market and host market growth.

A major complicating factor in the move abroad is the action of competitors. This type of reaction among large firms has been analysed as a major influence on a foreign direct investment. Among the largest multinational firms entry into particular host country markets is often grouped in time. The important influences on this are:

- industry structure: the more concentrated the industry, the more leader–follower behaviour occurs;
- industry stability: rivalistic investment behaviour is directly connected with the break-up of industry stability under pressure from new entrants;

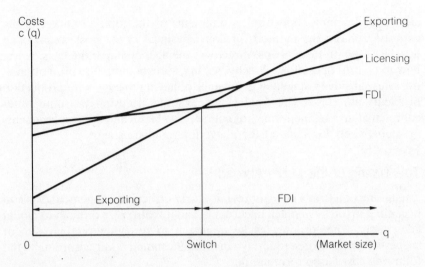

FIGURE 10.2   The timing of a foreign direct investment (FDI)
Note: In this example, licensing is never the preferred alternative.
Source: Reproduced from Peter J. Buckley and Mark Casson, *The Economic Theory of the Multinational Enterprise* (Macmillan, London, 1985), p. 105, with permission.

- the smaller the number of options open to the firm, the more likely they are to engage in oligopolistic reaction.

Interestingly, low-technology firms are defensively more active than high-technology ones.

10.3   FOREIGN MARKET SERVICING POLICIES

General

Foreign market servicing policies are the set of decisions which determine which production and service facilities serve particular markets and by what channels these are linked. There are three main modes of foreign market servicing: exporting, licensing (and other contractual arrangements) and foreign direct investment. Exporting can be differentiated from the other two methods because the bulk of value-adding activity takes place at home, while licensing can be differentiated because it is a market arrangement, not subject to complete internal control.

In practice, market servicing policy is highly complex. The methods are interrelated, i.e. location abroad of some activities will have knock-on effects across markets and products. Coordination of a foreign market servicing strategy is a major task. This is complicated by the fact that the optimum market servicing stance must alter as circumstances change, and a willingness to be flexible is vital.

Similar considerations apply to the sourcing network for inputs as an international procurement policy can be a major source of savings. Again, flexibility and monitoring of foreign operations are crucial.

Exporting

As figure 10.1 shows, exporting is often the primary means of penetrating a foreign market. It is regarded as a cheap and low-risk method of foreign selling, but the fixed costs of a low volume of export sales can be prohibitive despite the fact that there are tax advantages to be gained in many countries. The main problems of exporting are the costs of product adaptation and the difficulties caused by barriers to trade.

Research on exporting suggests that several elements are important in export success:

- the need for export sales specialists within the firm;
- the need to concentrate on the firm's most important foreign markets rather than amass haphazard uncoordinated foreign sales;
- the importance of selection, training and control of foreign intermediaries and effecting feedback from the foreign market.

Proper representation in the foreign market is vital, and the need to protect export markets by defensive investment in sales or production subsidiaries leads to a deepening involvement and further internationalization.

Licensing and Other Contractual Arrangements Abroad

On the face of it, foreign licensing appears to represent an ideal situation, combining the technological and possible management skills of the multinational firm with the local knowledge of the host country partner. The relatively small use of licensing, which represents only 7 per cent of the UK's total foreign sales,[4] is a result of the management difficulties of effecting the firm-to-firm transfer of technology and skills which imposes heavy costs, as compared to the internalization of such resources in the multinational firm's subsidiaries.[5] The problems involved in licensing include the following:

1 Identifying the advantage to be transferred which is related to the degree of embodiment of the technology. If the technology is embodied in a machine or a brand name then transfer is easy. Often, however, the skills of multinational firms are diffuse and involve heavy transfer costs.

2 Licensing technology involves heavy policing costs, for the licensor needs to ensure that the licensee does not use technology 'in ways which have not been paid for'.
3 The licensor runs the risk of creating a competitor.
4 There exists a 'buyer uncertainty problem' (the buyer does not know what he is acquiring until he has obtained it, and once he has acquired it he will not wish to pay for it) which inhibits the market for licences or at least increases the cost by requiring insurance clauses in contracts.
5 There may be no local firm which can profitably absorb the knowledge, particularly in less-developed countries.

However, there are a number of situations where licensing may be appropriate. First, it may pay multinationals in highly concentrated industries not to compete directly through subsidiaries in the same market, but to cross-license their products to each other (for instance, in the pharmaceutical industry). Secondly, licensing may be the best form of market servicing in the presence of barriers to the other methods. Government policy may prevent exporting and may insist on local host control. Small firms may find it difficult to raise the capital and management of a direct investment but require a local presence. Finally, licensing is often a way to exploit small, residual markets at low cost.

Direct Investment

Direct investment has been considered above. Three situations occur where management chooses direct foreign investment. First, firms move abroad by investment when the market growth or profit potential is favourable relative to other forms of market servicing. Secondly, firms produce abroad where their competitive strength is greater than indigenous firms. Thirdly, multinational firms are better seekers of the most profitable and fastest growing activities than are host country firms. One form of direct investment worthy of further investigation is cost-reducing offshore production.

Offshore Production

Offshore production is the situation where one stage in an integrated production process is located abroad in order to reduce costs. The offshore plant (or foreign feeder plant) is usually located in a cheap labour country and the final output is sold in an advanced country, usually in the multinational firm's home market. A typical offshore process is shown in figure 10.3.

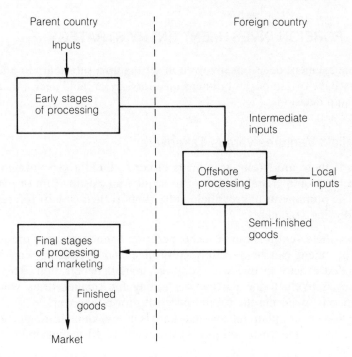

FIGURE 10.3   Schematic representation of a typical offshore
production process

In the electronics industry the most popular countries for offshore investment are Singapore, Malaysia, Hong Kong, Taiwan and South Korea; for servicing the US market, Latin America is popular, particularly Mexico; and for the European textiles market, North Africa.

The decision process leading to the establishment of an offshore plant is usually prompted by a threat to the home market from a low-cost producer. The threatened firm either has to reduce costs or phase out the product. Frequently offshore establishment is the optimum way to cut the costs. Successful establishment offshore is dependent on several characteristics of the product:

- large inputs of relatively unskilled labour;
- a high value to low weight ratio in order to keep transport costs down;
- low tariffs in the reimporting country;
- a standardized product and process.

Initial problems of offshore plants, such as inadequate throughput and difficulties of management at a distance, together with the inherent risks, have receded as managements have learned to cope, and offshore production is a rapidly increasing component of international investment.

10.4   FOREIGN INVESTMENT ENTRY STRATEGY

The management decisions involved in setting up a subsidiary in a foreign country have two important dimensions: the buy or build decision and the ownership decision.

Greenfield Ventures versus Takeovers

A priori, there are strong arguments either to build a new foreign plant from scratch on a greenfield site or to acquire an existing firm or part of a firm. The proponents of greenfield entry support their case by reference to the following arguments:

1   Greenfield ventures can be a cheaper form of entry because the scale of involvement can be precisely controlled and the facility can be expanded exactly in line with achieved market penetration. This argument is likely to be particularly strong for smaller firms who face difficulty in raising the capital necessary for a takeover.
2   Building a new plant means that there is no risk of inheriting problems.
3   The most modern techniques of production and management can be installed.
4   There is likely to be a welcome from the host government for greenfield ventures which are seen as increasing activity.
5   The choice of location is open to the entrant and a least-cost site, including possible regional grants, can be chosen.
6   Where no suitable takeover victim can be found, greenfield entry can be a second best solution.

There are counter arguments in favour of entry by takeover:

1   Takeovers permit rapid market entry and allow a quicker return on capital and learning procedures. In cases of strong competition, the pre-emption of a rival firm's move may dictate takeover entry.
2   Cultural, legal and management problems, particularly in the difficult start-up period, can be avoided by assimilating a going concern.
3   The major advantage of a takeover is often the purchase of crucial assets. Such assets may, in different circumstances, be products, management skills, brand names, technology and distribution networks.
4   Takeovers do not disturb the competitive framework in the host country, and they avoid competition retaliation.

There are, however, several potential drawbacks to the takeover mode of entry. The entrant is faced with the task of evaluating the worth of the assets to be acquired. This involves a costly and difficult assessment of the synergy between these new assets and the firm's existing operations. Secondly, there may be severe problems of integrating a previously independent unit into a larger entity; and, thirdly, the search for the ideal victim often involves heavy costs.

Almost every entry decision involves giving a different weighting to the above factors. Of particular importance in determining the outcome are the specific skills of the entrant and the environmental circumstances in the host country.

Ownership Strategy

The arguments for 100 per cent equity ownership of a foreign subsidiary rely heavily on the fact that control by the parent is total and that there can be no conflict over potentially contentious issues of company policy such as dividend payments, exports, the distribution of new investment and internal transfer prices. In cases where the parent firm can supply all the necessary inputs for a subsidiary, these costs of interference need not be borne. Further information, both technical and competitive, is not leaked to outsiders who may not fully share the goals of the parent firm. Finally, some types of strategy are incompatible with joint ventures, notably those based on rapid and sustained innovation, on rationalization and on control of key inputs.

The arguments for joint ventures are more circumstantial and depend on finding a joint venture partner with complementary resources. The argument that unique resources are contributed by the local partner is usually the most important reason for joint ventures. These resources may be local knowledge, contacts or marketing expertise. Secondly, the entrant company's outlay is reduced and the risk of loss correspondingly diminished. This reduction of risk is an important reason why joint ventures, which can be easily reversed, may be a good way of effecting initial entry. Finally, in many countries some element of local shareholding is made a condition of entry.

The success of the decision to enter a joint venture will, of course, depend on the choice of partner. There are many cases on record where a good agent or distributor has become a poor joint venture partner. It is clearly difficult to appraise a prospective partner in advance, but on such an appraisal may depend the success of the foreign venture.

10.5 MANAGEMENT IN MULTINATIONAL FIRMS

Management in multinational firms is essentially a response to the same issues facing national firms: how to make a profit; how to control operations; how and in which direction to grow; how to respond to a changing environment and so on; but it is complicated by operating in more than one country and by differing national business frameworks. Consequently, each functional area of the firm – financing, marketing, production, R&D – must be organized so as to respond to global operations.

Organization

Organizationally, the multinational firm must respond to global challenges in a way which allows the maximum control of policy by top decision-makers with maximum flexibility of response to changing circumstances. This means the creation of an efficient communications network within the firm. Reporting relationships between managers is therefore vital. Channels of reporting relationships internationally can run along functional lines, where the heads of divisions (finance, marketing, production) have worldwide responsibilities, along product group lines, or the firm can be organized geographically (Middle East division etc.). The organizational problem then becomes the effective coordination of these major divisions across the other specialism, e.g. in a product division structure to coordinate the sales of different product groups. Some multinational firms have thus adopted multiple reporting channels (sometimes referred to as matrix structures). Here the danger is that the organizational procedures may become disorientated.

An alternative response to global organization, particularly utilized by smaller multinationals, is the International Division structure, where all non-domestic activities of the firm are grouped together and reporting is directly between the Chief Executive of the company and the Chief Executive of the International Division. Such a structure is useful in giving impetus to an internationalization drive, but does not allow the firm to benefit fully from synergy between national and international operations and often leaves foreign activities dependent on the domestic product division.

Personnel problems in multinational firms can be severe. Expatriate executives are far more expensive than when employed at home and pose problems in promotion, pensions, emoluments and reintegration at home. Recruitment of local executives can be difficult and risky but may be forced on the company by indigenization plans, by which local governments demand that a fixed proportion of executives must be host country nationals. Cultural differences among executives often require careful handling by top management. A training programme which matches these personnel needs is a vital component of a multinational's operations.

Planning

It has become commonplace that structure should follow strategy, and the setting of strategy at the highest levels – the management plan – is a vital weapon in the economic management of multinationals. Three elements are of major importance:

- control of operations;
- decision-making by the people best equipped to judge the impact of the decision;
- the communication of information to facilitate good decisions.

The management plan should thus incorporate well-defined targets which can be measured. Multiple targets which are comprehensible to decision-makers should include a time-scale for their achievement and an action programme to tackle key problems and take advantage of opportunities. Such provisions prevent the plan being vague and give clear guidance to managers.

The key issue of developing responsibility to the managers of foreign subsidiaries while retaining control of policy in headquarters is an issue which troubles all multinational firms, however organized. It is essential that group support be given to the manager on the spot who must actually make operational decisions.

Financial Planning

Multinational operation complicates financial management by posing extra problems, but it also opens new opportunities. The possibilities for exchange loss or gain increase with multinationalization. Exchange loss is the risk of loss to a firm exposed to devaluation in the value of a currency which the firm is contracted to receive in the future or from an appreciation in the value of a currency which the firm is contracted to deliver in the future. Exporters and importers are so exposed, but multinationals are more vulnerable because of their larger trading across exchanges and because their net assets will be differentially affected in different currency areas. Consequently, a hedging policy designed to minimize these effects is necessary for a risk-averse multinational. Of course, a more aggressive policy of attempting to play the foreign exchange market is a possible alternative, but no such scheme has yet been perfected and many multinational firms have lost money in the attempt.

The differential cost of money worldwide enables multinational firms to reduce the costs of raising capital, and the use of internal indebtedness (e.g. a subsidiary borrowing from the parent firm) allows flexibility in its utilization. However, each subsidiary of the firm must adapt to local financial practices and institutions. The reconciliation of local subsidiaries into an overall consolidated balance sheet can be a difficult and expensive task.

Financial planning in the multinational firm must face the issue of taxation. A spectrum of policies is possible from an outright policy of attempting to reduce taxation payments wherever possible to ensuring simply that the same profits are not taxed twice. A large amount of information on tax regimes and double taxation agreements between countries is necessary in international taxation planning and a great deal of uncertainty prevails because of the impact of changes in any of the variables affecting taxation.

The problem of withdrawing funds from abroad is a unique financial problem faced by multinational firms. A variety of channels is available including dividends (usually taxed at source and as income to the parent), royalties and management fees to the parent (often tax-deductible in the host country), repayment of loans and interest on intra-company debt, and transfer pricing on intermediate goods and services.

The problem of transfer pricing is the most controversial issue that multinational firms face. The manipulation of internal prices of goods and services to move funds around the world can achieve several objectives. Included among these are the following:

● to maximize post-tax profits;
● artificially to affect declared profit levels;
● to transfer funds in the face of changes in currency parities;
● to avoid government restrictions;
● to impose control on foreign subsidiaries.

However, such artificial prices affect the incomes of the countries between which the transaction occurs and multinationals are therefore distrusted by governments who believe that they cannot control their own economies in the presence of multinational firms. Despite the existence of constraints by customs and revenue authorities, exchange control authorities and special-ist transfer price checking firms employed by some countries, suspicion remains. The practice also has drawbacks from the firm's point of view. A loss of efficiency can occur from the operation of non-market prices. A costly control system may be necessary and mistakes in transfer pricing may be expensive. The practice will continue, however, while potential gains in tax avoidance and profit potential remain.

The existence of different tax and trading regimes internationally poses the problem of evaluating the performance of foreign subsidiaries. While it is generally agreed that the same standards of performance (return on sales, performance relative to a budget) are required from individual foreign subsidiaries, allowance must be made for the impact of local conditions and possibly the impact of transfer pricing on individual subsidiaries. Evaluation of performance at a distance remains a grey area in many multinational firms.

Marketing

International marketing involves an important decision on worldwide standardization versus adaptation of the products to individual market needs. In general, adaptation will yield revenue advantages. It is, however, dangerous to make generalizations, particularly in equating market with country. India, for instance, though a very poor country on the usual indicators, has a proportionately small but, in absolute terms, large industrial sector. Most Third World countries have a minority of high-income earners whose consumption patterns approximate to those of advanced countries. Consequently, multinationals are often able to segment national markets profitably.

Studies of international marketing point to the importance of non-price factors in selling. Quality, variety, reliability and meeting delivery dates are frequently adduced to lead to success in penetrating foreign markets. Information needs are correspondingly greater in foreign markets and careful pre-entry market research remains an important contributor to success.

Research and Development

Economic theories of the multinational firm stress the relationship between research intensity and multinationality of the firm. The supply of technological advances internally exploited and marketed within the structure of the firm gives an explanation for the growth of integrated multinational firms.[6] The management of R&D is vital for internationalization, and exploiting the advances of internal research provides a motor for the growth of the firm. The information flows between R&D and the other main functions are extremely important. Figure 10.4 illustrates the two-way communication necessary for management to integrate fully the fruits of research into the management process. It is often argued that the most successfully managed multinationals are those whose managements understand the implications of current research.

Global Decision-making

The management of multinational firms requires a careful monitoring of the international environment. Responsiveness to local conditions is perhaps the most important attribute of successful management practice.

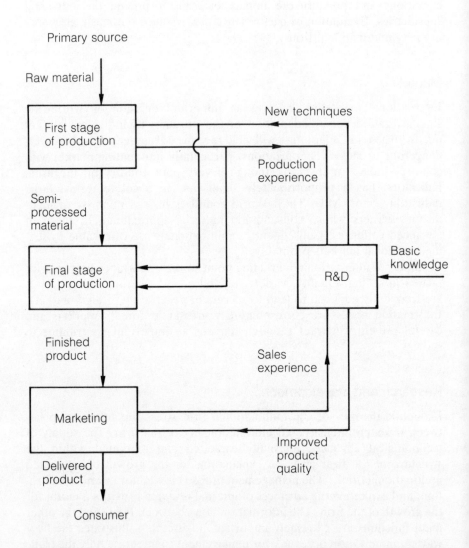

FIGURE 10.4   The integration of R&D into the management of the firm
Note: Successive stages of production are linked by flows of semi-processed materials. Production and marketing are linked by a flow of finished goods ready for distribution. They are linked to R&D by two-way flows of information and expertise
Source: Reproduced from Peter J. Buckley and Mark Casson *The Future of the Multinational Enterprise* (2nd edn, Macmillan, London, 1991), p. 34, with permission.

This section has shown the crucial importance of communication within the firm not only between countries, but between departments and divisions.

10.6 THE RELATIONSHIP WITH THE ENVIRONMENT

Multinational firms operate in more than one economic environment and therefore have to adapt to local conditions, markets and jurisdictions. Further, they must coordinate activities which operate on very different bases because of different local influences.

The Host Country Environment

Understanding and adapting to foreign conditions remains a difficult problem even for the most experienced multinational firm. Different ways of conducting business and changing regulatory regimes impose learning and adaptation costs. The assessment of such costs in advance of entry can be problematic. In particular, multinationals are faced with the assessment of political risk, which is usually discounted in the home environment. Political risks arise from discontinuities in the business environment which are difficult to predict. War, revolution, nationalization, expropriation, devaluation and the imposition of controls are obvious manifestations. Collection of information is necessary to evaluate foreign projects and a variety of screening models exists. Prior contact with the market is an important source of knowledge of host country conditions.

In many host countries, notably those of the Third World, multinationals are regarded with suspicion and they are often made the scapegoat for many internal problems of economic management. Concern on the part of host countries is expressed with regard to the impact of multinationals on the balance of payments, their effect on the host country's economic structure, their technological impact and their alleged inflexibility towards national planning. Indeed, it is frequently the case that foreign investors are more responsive to government policy than are local firms, and the alacrity with which multinationals respond to regional incentives is an example of this. However, the vague threat posed to national sovereignty and the achievement of national goals dictates that the management of multinationals must be sensitive to local aspirations and must avoid at all costs political interference or standards of behaviour below those of their best local competitor.

The Source Country

The relationship between the multinational firm and its source country can also be fraught with difficulty. The most serious accusation thrown at multinationals is that they create unemployment by 'exporting jobs'. The growth of offshore production in particular has heightened the tension. In defence, multinationals put the view that foreign investment increases job provision in the home country by providing an outlet for intermediate and capital goods in the foreign unit and preserving jobs which would otherwise disappear in the face of low-cost foreign competition. Studies of the balance between job preservation and job loss conducted in the USA have been inconclusive, as have investigations of the impact of outward direct investment on the balance of payments.

International Organizations

Because of the difficulty of controlling multinational firms at the national level, demands have grown that they should be internationally (or supranationally) regulated. To effect this a number of codes of conduct and other regulatory provisions now impinge on the management of multinational firms.

Clearly, managements in multinationals must be aware of these codes and adopt policies which do not conflict with them for the sake of public relations, if nothing else. The impact of international regulation is likely to increase and therefore to impose management costs on multinationals much more heavily in future.

10.7 CONCLUSION

The management of multinational organizations has additional dimensions not faced by the national firm. Adaptation to differing local conditions, extra information requirements, control problems, organizational problems and problems of liaising with external decision-makers are all exacerbated by international operations. However, with these problems come opportunities for growth, stability, diversification and cost reduction, leading to higher profitability. The principles of sound management do not differ between national and international firms, but the extra dimensions of the latter pose interesting challenges.

10.8 MANAGEMENT SUMMARY AND CHECKLIST

1   What is the objective of investing abroad? Is it cost reduction, more effective servicing of demand or control of key supplies?
2   Have all the other means of servicing a foreign market been considered and evaluated? Is a form of licensing, exporting or foreign investment

the most appropriate means of reaching the target market? Have other markets been assessed?

3   Has the most efficient supply (sourcing) network been established for all the units of the company, at home and abroad?

4   Has the entry into the foreign market been evaluated correctly? Is a greenfield site or takeover entry most appropriate? If acquisition is preferred, are all the potential acquisition targets fully evaluated? Is the ownership strategy matched to the objectives and to the resources available?

5   Are foreign units organized in such a way that reporting and control is flexible and efficient? Are decision-making units by function, area and product coordinated? Are local managers clear about their responsibilities?

6   Are conditions in the (actual and potential) host countries fully monitored and reported back to the key decision-makers?

7   Does the firm operate on a truly international basis, scanning opportunities, appraising and re-appraising its global spread and fully coordinating its activities on a worldwide basis?

NOTES

1   Peter J. Buckley, Gerald D. Newbould and Jane Thurwell, *Foreign Direct Investment by Smaller UK Firms* (2nd edn, Macmillan, London, 1988).

2   Raymond Vernon, 'International Investment and International Trade in the Product Cycle', *Quarterly Journal of Economics*, 80 (1966), pp.196–207.

3   Peter J. Buckley and Mark Casson, *The Economic Theory of the Multinational Enterprise* (Macmillan, London, 1985).

4   Peter J. Buckley and Kate Prescott, 'The Structure of British Industry's Sales in Foreign Markets', *Managerial and Decision Economics*, 10 (1989), pp.189–208.

5   Buckley and Casson, *The Economic Theory of the Multinational Enterprise;* Peter J. Buckley and Mark Casson, *The Future of the Multinational Enterprise* (2nd edn, Macmillan, London, 1990).

6   Buckley and Casson, *The Future of the Multinational Enterprise*.

FURTHER READING

For a thorough treatment of the management policies of multinational firms see: Michael Z. Brooke and Peter J. Buckley (eds) *Handbook of International Trade* (Macmillan, London, 1988).

11 Strategies for Declining Industries

Introduction—What is a Declining Industry?—Reasons
for Product Decline—Factors Leading to Success or
Failure—Strategies for Declining Industries—
Management Summary and Checklist

11.1 INTRODUCTION

In retrospect, examples of and reasons for the decline in the demand for
products are easily identifiable. The demand for blacksmith's services was
overtaken by the advent of the internal combustion engine, chimney
sweeps experienced a decline in the demand for their services with the
widespread adoption of central heating as the primary means for home
heating and, more recently, the Swiss watch industry has suffered a decline
resulting from changes in electronic engineering.

Until the oil crises in the middle and late 1970s the increasing rate of
growth of GNP and world trade had resulted in increases in demand for
many products which had continued for an unprecedented period of time.
These crises and the consequent reduction in economic activity, together
with the increasing rate of technological change, resulted in more products
facing a period of long-term decline. Long-term decline is not a new
phenomenon in the industrial environment and the concept of product
life-cycle provides the theoretical explanation of this observed reality.
However, little attention had previously been focused on this part of the
cycle. A simple view was that a product in a declining market was
undesirable, so that such products should be eliminated from the portfolio
as soon as possible and, furthermore, entry to such markets or products
was a strategy to be avoided.

It is against this background that Harrigan, building on Porter's model,
undertook some research on products in declining industries and subse-
quently developed a conceptual framework which sought to outline
strategies which would be profitable for companies with products in such
industries.[1] Also, it is argued from the BCG matrix (chapter 14) that

companies need a balanced portfolio of businesses. It follows, therefore, that developing appropriate strategies for declining products is of major importance to the performance of most businesses.

It is often difficult for senior managers to accept that a product is in the decline phase. They may have been in the industry or associated with the product for many years. Also acceptance of the situation might indicate the need for substantial change to be introduced: new products, new customers, new processes and so on. Managers may have a tendency to ignore these factors and refuse to face the facts such that profitability can be seriously affected and even the existence of the firm threatened. The strategies required to cope with seriously *underperforming* companies are discussed in chapter 12.

11.2 WHAT IS A DECLINING INDUSTRY?

It will be useful to discuss two situations which are often confused with a declining industry. Figure 11.1 helps to illustrate the point.

Although the product life-cycle is usually drawn as a continuous smooth line, the reality is that sales fluctuate in the short term due to cyclical or other short-run influences. The first illusion which is sometimes believed is that any reduction in sales is a product in a declining industry. It is

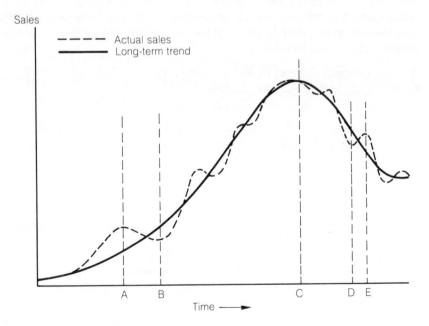

FIGURE 11.1   The product life-cycle

apparent that, although sales are declining between points A and B, this is a temporary decline in what in the long term is a growing industry. Likewise, the second illusion which is too often accepted is that a temporary increase, as for instance between D and E, is evidence that the industry is now in a new growth phase. Of course, it may be, but in figure 11.1 this is only a short-term reprieve in what is clearly a long-term decline. An industry is in decline after it has reached point C on the diagram.

From this point in the cycle onwards there must be, by definition, excess capacity, that is, demand at a lower point than maximum output. Economic theory suggests that certain features of industry behaviour will result from this excess capacity such as price wars which are initially designed to increase sales in order to maintain full plant utilization. Also, companies leave the industry as the marginal producer is no longer able to operate profitably. However, there are other options and whether or not these are possible are discussed at a later point in the chapter.

11.3 REASONS FOR PRODUCT DECLINE

Causes of declining profitability are also mentioned in chapter 12, 'Corporate Collapse and Turnaround'. As that chapter is concerned with under-performance whatever the state of demand, the discussion focuses on issues *within* the company. As the focus of this chapter is declining industry demand it is appropriate to focus on the *external* factors which have led to decline. The major factors are:

- technological change: to products or processes
- social changes: cultural or fashion
- saturation: buyers have sufficient quantities of the product.

There may be other factors, such as a new law or economic policy, but these are often preceded by one of the above factors. Also, changes may be a combination of two or all three factors. The demise of the corner shop and the growth in the number of supermarkets results from a wide range of social and technological changes.

A new technical process or source, e.g. natural gas, can cause the decline of a product, e.g. manufactured gas. There is a growing need for fuel but it is being provided by a different process. The introduction of powerful computer systems has reduced the demand for cash registers. A new technology has produced a product which has changed and subsumed the task of the register to meet a much wider range of customer needs. Changes in fashion in the men's clothing market have seen a significant decline in the demand for suits, and social changes such as a fall in the birthrate have caused a substantial decline in the baby products market.

Most companies operate successfully within given geographical areas and excursions into new territory are often met with fierce resistance. Thus, given this geographical limitation many markets reach saturation, that is they reach a peak when demand has been fully satisfied and there then follows a fall until, at a lower point, sales level out to satisfy the replacement market. Televisions, refrigerators and other household goods fall into this category in the UK. Of course, if the population were rising rapidly this trend might be different.

11.4   FACTORS LEADING TO SUCCESS OR FAILURE

The models used by strategists for choosing between alternative courses of action (chapter 14) are based on an external and an internal dimension or dimensions and the model described in this chapter elaborates on a particular aspect of those models. As with the multinational firm (chapter 10) and corporate collapse and turnaround (chapter 12), the specific insights into these critical areas are considered in part III so that the resulting analysis can be carried through the process into part IV which can then focus solely on how the choice is made for the standard case. It is necessary, therefore, to outline the key external and internal features before suggesting the possible options which may be appropriate for a given set of circumstances.

Environmental Factors

Environmental factors can be classified under two headings:

* demand characteristics
* supply characteristics.

Demand characteristics are those factors which relate to the customers for the product. Outlined below are some of the key issues.

Nature of decline

The nature of the fall in demand for the industry's product is most often the key demand factor. If demand is falling slowly, this is preferable to rapid decline. Indeed, in the latter case it could be at such a rate as to render further analysis unneccessary. As well as the rate of decline, the pattern of decline is significant: steady decline being preferable to volatile decline. Also it is important in making such estimates of future demand to understand the reasons for the decline.

Industry structure

The number and size of competitors and their relative market share will enable some preliminary assessment of the nature of competition in the industry. A few large buyers is likely to lead to increased pressure on the industry unless there is some countervailing power such as a patent, few alternatives or expensive costs in switching among suppliers.

Price stability

The nature of decline and industry structure will be key factors in determining whether price stability will be maintained in the market. Falling or unstable prices are an unfavourable industry characteristic.

Product differentiation

In general, when a product reaches the decline stage of the life-cycle it is or is becoming commodity-like with no perceived differences between the products of competing companies. This is an unfavourable characteristic but not always a bar to operating successfully in the industry. However, differentiation between products does provide more opportunities.

Segments

There can be a number of segments within an industry. Each segment may contain commodity-like or differentiated products. The existence of different segments is a positive factor, in that it is likely that there will be among them pockets of demand which are not declining as rapidly as others.

The second class of external characteristics are those that relate to the companies that manufacture or *supply* the product or service which comprises the industry. Before outlining specific issues, it is necessary to discuss the general problems associated with exit and entry barriers. Either singly or in combination, several of the factors outlined below can constitute barriers. Exit barriers are circumstances, such as assets significantly overvalued in the accounts, which would create major problems should the company decide to stop operating in that business. Likewise, although entry is not often appropriate at this stage of the cycle, barriers to entry will enable those currently in the industry to manage the decline phase in an orderly manner without threat from outside interference.

Level of excess capacity

To some extent the levels of excess capacity are linked to the rate of decline but they are also a function of the increases in productivity in the industry and the rate at which firms leave the industry. High levels of excess capacity are usually extremely unfavourable, but individual firms may not be as affected as others if operating in particular segments.

Vertical integration

If firms in the supplying industry are vertically integrated there will be a greater reluctance to leave the industry. Vertical integration is therefore an unattractive industry feature.

Industry structure

An industry comprising a few large suppliers with large market share is likely to result in more orderly management of the decline in demand than an industry comprising a large number of small suppliers each with small market share.

Company ownership

Where ownership is with a large corporation decisions are likely to be made on a more rational and dispassionate basis, so that a business not reaching or likely to reach a given rate of return on capital is likely to be closed or divested. However, in the one-product or single-owner company survival at any cost may result in a continuation in business until, in some cases, bankruptcy occurs. An industry therefore comprising single-product or single-owner businesses is not attractive.

Asset characteristics

Companies whose assets are in the account at significantly greater value than are realizable in resale terms whether as a divestment or after closure are going to be reluctant to leave the industry. Also, in industries where company assets have no alternative use. Thus an industry is unattractive in which this is the situation for several of the companies.

Company Strengths and Weaknesses

The general approach to determining company strengths and weaknesses has been outlined in chapters 7 and 8 and many factors relevant to declining demand may emerge from such an analysis. However, four factors are worthy of particular note.

Management attitudes

The perceptions the management have of the features of the industry and their reactions to them will be critical in determining the way in which the decline phase proceeds. As mentioned previously, managements often have long attachments to products and markets which mean that they experienced the products while in their growth phase. Failure to perceive, acknowledge and adapt to the changed circumstances can have serious consequences. Although this factor has been included in the internal dimension of the analysis, the collective perceptions and actions of all firms in the industry are very important and give the process a potential dynamic which makes it very difficult to predict the outcome. However, early and appropriate action is likely to bring greater success to the company.

Market share

A business which has a large market share is in a more favourable position than one with a low market share. This applies to the whole industry or individual segments.

Cost position in the industry

A feature of declining industries is the inevitability that at some point the highest-cost producer will have to exit. Also, if prices are squeezed, then the higher-cost producers' profitability will decline. Accordingly, those who are lower-cost producers have a competitive advantage.

Patents

At this stage of the cycle it is possible that patents which have protected products from competition may be near expiry date. If this is so then the impact of the loss of protection needs to be carefully evaluated. The more severe the likely competitive impact the less attractive to companies in the industry.

Before discussing the possible strategies, a number of points need to be made as a summary of the preceding analysis and as an introduction to the model. The factors mentioned above are those which are found to be the most significant in determining future strategy. On occasion, factors not mentioned here may be of critical importance and it is the skill and experience of the analyst that will enable those factors to be identified and included in the analyses. Also, it has to be borne in mind constantly that this analysis is concerned with declining demand.

Thus, the model outlined below may also be appropriate where demand has reached an equilibrium but is *definitely not appropriate for other points on the product life-cycle*. Finally, these are general rules to which there will be exceptions. Thus, again, the analyst needs acute sensitivity to identify when a general rule is not applicable.

11.5   STRATEGIES FOR DECLINING INDUSTRIES

From the two dimensions outlined in the previous section (11.4), environmental factors and company strengths and weaknesses, it is possible to contruct a simple model (figure 11.2) with one on each axis. Although the model has apparently four discrete cells, it should be noted that each axis is in reality continuous so that the divisions are to facilitate analysis. It can be seen that the strongest position is the top left-hand corner of the diagram: considerable strengths in an industry with a large number of favourable traits. It follows, therefore, that the bottom right-hand corner is the worst possible situation. Thus, as the product is positioned in this diagram so the strategy most likely to succeed is indicated. The bands for the four

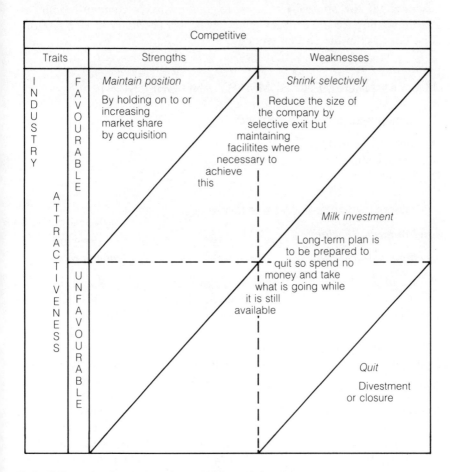

FIGURE 11.2   Strategies for declining industries

strategies are drawn diagonally across the diagram to complement the favourable (top left) to unfavourable (bottom right) axis:

- Maintain position: maintain facilities by holding or increasing market share by acquisition.
- Shrink selectively: reduce the size of the company by selective exit but maintaining facilities where necessary to achieve this.
- Milk investment: long-term plan is to be prepared to quit so spend no money and take what is going while it is still available.
- Quit: divestment or closure.

There is a danger that models explained in two-dimensional planes may be intepreted as static, whereas the reality is of a constant state of change as companies merge, close down or make new competitive moves. Thus, it is essential for the strategist to seek to identify likely competitive moves before settling for a particular policy. It is also necessary to evaluate the inherent risks in the chosen strategy.

11.6   MANAGEMENT SUMMARY AND CHECKLIST

1   Reasons for decline in demand

- technological change
- social change
- market saturation.

2   Factors leading to success or failure

Environmental Factors:

Demand characteristics	Favourable	Unfavourable
Nature of the decline	Slow speed	Rapid
	Steady	Volatile
Industry structure	Supplier power	Buyer power
Price stability	Stable	Fluctuating/falling
Product differentiation	Differentiated	Commodity-like
Segments	Some segments	No segments

Supply Characteristics

Level of excess capacity	Low	High
Vertical integration	Significant	Non-existent
Industry structure	Few suppliers	Many suppliers
Company ownership	Part of large corporation	Dominated by owners

Asset characteristics	Undervalued Alternative uses	Overvalued No alternative uses
Company strengths and weaknesses:	*Strength*	*Weakness*
Management attitudes	Knowledge of situation	Misperception or failure to acknowledge situation
Market share	High	Low
Cost position in industry	Low	High
Patent	Some time before expiry	None/nearly expired

3 Strategies for declining industries

- maintain position
- shrink selectively
- milk investment
- quit.

NOTE

1 M. E. Porter, *Competitive Strategy and Competitive Advantage* (Free Press, Glencoe, 1980 and 1985); K. R. Harrigan, *Strategies for Declining Businesses* (Lexington Books, Lexington, Mass., 1980).

12 Corporate Collapse and Turnaround

Symptoms of Decline—Causes of Decline—Feasibility of Recovery—Strategies for Recovery—Management Summary and Checklist

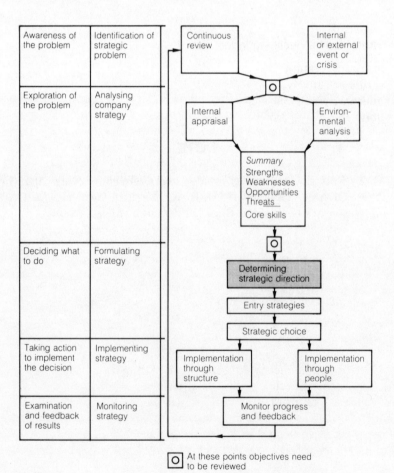

FIGURE 12.1   The strategic decision-making process

Chapter 9 provided a means of determining the future direction of a business. However, it is possible that as a result of falling profitability, strategy is so constrained that policies adopted are focused on offsetting the threats and/or eliminating the weaknesses which have led to the falling profitability. This is a situation which will arise in most companies from time to time, and research is now beginning to supply helpful insights into the processes of decline and recovery or, in some cases, collapse. This chapter will therefore be concerned with the symptoms and causes of decline, the feasibility of recovery and the strategic policies required for recovery where recovery is possible.

12.1 SYMPTOMS OF DECLINE

What is 'decline'? As with many other aspects of business policy, there is, as yet, no definitive answer to this question. Basically, a company in decline is one in which there is some doubt concerning the survival of the company. As a fundamental reason for the collapse of most companies is their inability to produce sufficient profit, a simple definition of decline is falling profitability, measured by falling returns on capital employed or earnings per share. Another dimension of decline is the time span over which decline has occurred. While accurate prediction is rarely possible, declining profitability does not usually occur without some previous indications. For example, in figure 12.2, the first example would be occasioned by some exceptional event, for instance an acquisition which 'went wrong'. The second example indicates the more likely pattern, that is that a period of declining profitability is preceded by a period of no growth and a period when the rate of growth is decreasing. Accurate prediction is difficult because the time scale over which decline takes place may vary considerably. Also, it is often difficult to decide whether a reduction in the rate of growth is a temporary and insignificant occurrence or evidence of a more fundamental problem.

Symptoms and causes are in some cases closely connected, but the objective of this section is to provide some indicators which will help to identify potential crises. As with human illness, not all symptoms may be apparent in all cases, so with corporate illness all the symptoms of decline may not be in evidence in all companies experiencing declining profitability. Symptoms of decline are generally evident in the finance and marketing figures. The most obvious financial indications are a reduction in dividends, increasing debt and decreasing liquidity. Significant research efforts here have been devoted to the prediction of decline and collapse through the use of financial models.[1] However, while these may give some general indication of the health of a business, their ability to predict bankruptcy with any overall degree of accuracy is extremely doubtful, both

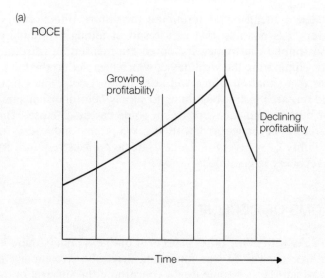

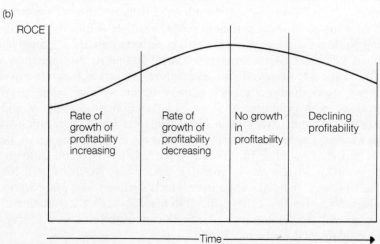

FIGURE 12.2   Patterns in declining profitability

on the basis of the methodology used[2] and also on the results obtained. In marketing terms, declining profitability may arise where there is no real increase in sales or where market share is falling.

12.2   CAUSES OF DECLINE

It could be argued that there is only one cause of declining profitability – bad management. If management were adequately tracking the success of its products and the changes which are likely to take place in their markets and were taking appropriate action, then profits would not decline. However, as such success would require omniscience (and given that few are prophets) even the most systematic managers will make mistakes. This section will therefore discuss those aspects of the interface between the business and its environment which result in declining profitability. The answers can be separated into those which are internal and those which are external to the firm (see table 12.1).

TABLE 12.1   Causes of declining profitability

Internal factors	External factors
Poor management	Declining demand for the product
Weaknesses in the finance function	Changes in the industry structure
Weaknesses in the marketing function	General economic, social or political factors
Weaknesses in the production/ operations function	
Mistaken acquisition	
Problems with a 'big' project	

Poor Management

All problems start at the top, and so poor management is the key to declining profitability. Those responsible for the operations of the company are making wrong decisions with respect either to the strategic decisions which are being made or to the personnel being employed to implement those decisions. The role and style of the chief executive (CEO) are critical. A major feature of corporate collapse is the autocratic style of leadership of the CEO. This is often evident when the role of chairman and chief executive are not separated and the board is not genuinely participating in the strategic decision-making process. While some flamboyant entrepreneurs succeed for a period of time, their style often leads to major problems and sometimes to bankruptcy. Recent examples include Freddie Laker and Clive Sinclair. Poor management can also result from an unbalanced board of directors; for example, too many accountants or engineers. Another reason can be lack of depth; that is, insufficient senior management resources either in terms of quantity or quality.

Finance

Poor financial control is often a cause of falling profitability. This can result from poor budgetary control, an inadequate costing system or an inability to monitor and control cash. Other weaknesses in the finance function can arise from faulty valuation of assets and creative accounting. A major reason for the demise of many small companies is overtrading, which may arise in several forms. The most frequently occurring is when the profit from increased turnover is insufficient to finance the money borrowed in order to expand.

Marketing

An inadequate marketing function will occur in those firms which fail fully to understand and operationalize the concept of marketing. Marketing is often an inappropriate term for the activity concerned. It is regularly used for selling, advertising or distribution. The evidence of real marketing activity in an organization stems from a marketing plan which guides the whole of the company/customer relationship and will be heavily dependent on marketing research information and the generation of new product-market offerings. Companies in decline have usually failed to embrace the marketing concept in these terms.

Production/Operations

A feature of the production function found in companies with declining profitability is a high cost structure relative to other manufacturers in the same industry. This might result from inefficient production methods or from poor labour relations leading to strikes.

Acquisition Policy

For some companies, an acquisition which has failed to generate the expected returns has been a major cause of corporate decline. The benefits expected from acquisition and the reasons why these are not always forthcoming are discussed in detail in chapter 13.

Big Projects

The 'big project' is another reason which sometimes causes declining profitability or collapse. By definition, the 'big project' represents an activity that is large in terms of company resources and which is likely significantly to affect profitability one way or another. The 'project' might be a large acquisition, a major capital investment in a new process or product, a major marketing campaign or substantial expenditure on research and development.

Declining Industry Sales

The most significant factor in the external environment is a fall in the demand for the product manufactured by the company: declining industry sales. It is important to identify whether this is part of a temporary economic recession or whether it is the beginning of a long-term trend. Also, the rate of decline and the reasons for decline are key factors when considering what action should be taken to restore profitability.

Industry Structure

Changes to the industry structure may also cause profitability to decline. For example if, in an industry where there are three major firms, two of them merge, then the third company may be put at a considerable disadvantage. The concentration and nature of competition in an industry will be key determinants of profitability

Other Environmental Factors

There are changes taking place in the economic, social, political and technological environments which will influence company performance. Occasionally some feature of these environments (discussed in detail in chapter 5) has a major impact on a specific industry or company. For instance, changes to commodity prices can have a significant effect on heavy users of a particular commodity. Likewise, changes in the exchange rate or some change in fashion or technology may have a devastating impact on profitability.

12.3   FEASIBILITY OF RECOVERY

The causes of decline are a synthesis of research on corporate collapse, turnaround and managing in a declining industry. A key question for companies with falling profitability is: is recovery possible? There are several features of such situations which enable the analyst to make some assessment concerning the feasibility of recovery.

It has been suggested by Argenti that corporate collapse is the end of a gradual period of decline during which profitability begins to fall and an increasing number of the causes for decline are evident or growing in significance.[3] The concept of declining profitability and the likelihood of recovery are illustrated in figure 12.3.

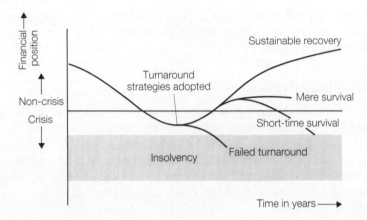

FIGURE 12.3   Types of recovery situation
Source: Stuart Slatter, *Corporate Recovery* (Penguin, Harmondsworth, 1984).
Reprinted with permission.

The objective of all companies which are in decline is to achieve a
long-term recovery. However, as profitability falls, it will become increasingly difficult to achieve this objective because the extent of the mismatch
between the products of the company and the markets served widens.
Once crisis level is reached, short-term solutions are often necessary, for
instance, selling assets to raise cash, which may have detrimental long-term
effects. 'Mere survival' and 'sustainable recovery' are ends of a continuous
scale of post-crisis profitability rather than two discrete groups into which
recovery companies can be categorized.

Harrigan suggests that there are two key dimensions for determining the
strategy and assessing performance in a declining industry:

- favourable or unfavourable industry characteristics;
- relative strengths and weaknesses of the business.[4]

These would be evaluated by a detailed analysis of the causes for decline.
Slatter used a similar classification, as shown in figure 12.4.[5]

12.4   STRATEGIES FOR RECOVERY

Action which may be taken to restore the ailing firm to profitability can be
considered in five groups:

- organizational changes
- finance and financial strategies
- cost-reduction strategies

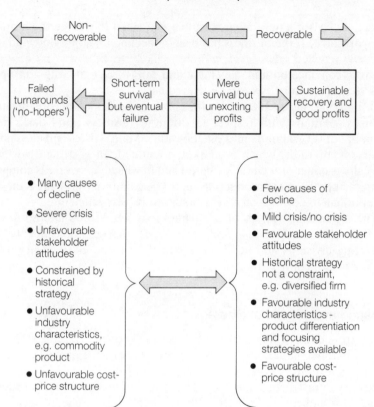

FIGURE 12.4   Factors determining the feasibility of recovery
Source: Stuart Slatter, *Corporate Recovery* (Penguin, Harmondsworth, 1984). Reprinted with permission

- asset-reduction strategies
- revenue-generating strategies.

Organizational Changes

In many turnaround situations, a key feature of the recovery is the appointment of a new chief executive (CEO) or other changes in the senior management of the company. In some cases the new CEO may be a company director who is a person with skills that can effect a return to profitability. As well as making appropriate strategic decisions, such new appointments need to change the working environment within the company. This can be achieved by attention to the ability and motivation of senior staff. Early decisions should be made on which staff, if any, need to be replaced and incentives need to be introduced in order to achieve given objectives. Also, a new chief executive may need to change the morale of the workforce. If the business has been in decline for some time and if this has now reached crisis level, morale is likely to be low. The new CEO needs to convince both management and workforce that, with appropriate new strategies, the crisis can be overcome.

It may be necessary to institute some fundamental organizational changes, perhaps with respect to different business units (such as the grouping of several units into one division). Many UK companies have an 'overseas' division, which is market orientated, in a structure which is basically product or technology based and in which the overseas companies manufacture the same products as their UK counterparts. Unless there are exceptionally good reasons this is likely to be less efficient.

The internal operations of companies may need to be altered to offset conflicts and weaknesses, and it is likely that relationships between operating divisions and head office will need to be clarified in terms of authority and control procedures.

Finance and Financial Strategies

The introduction of financial controls is usually one of the first steps taken in a turnaround situation because in many cases poor financial control has been a contributory cause of the decline in profitability. Also, it is often necessary to restructure the debt. This involves an agreement between the ailing firm and its creditors, usually the banks, to reschedule and sometimes convert interest and other principal payments into other negotiable financial instruments. Examples are the conversion of short-term into long-term debt or the conversion of loans into convertible preference shares or equity.

Cost-reduction Strategies

In severe crisis situations, cost-reduction strategies are often implemented at an early stage, as many will have an almost immediate effect. The management needs to examine which are the key areas of cost and to attend to those in the first instance. In many companies the key cost element is labour; that is, wages and salaries. An immediate effect can be achieved by banning overtime and stopping new recruitment. In the longer term it may be necessary to reduce the size of the labour force. This can be achieved through natural wastage, early retirement, voluntary redundancy or, if necessary, compulsory redundancy. The severity of the crisis will determine the speed with which the shedding of labour will need to be effected.

In some businesses the materials used in production can constitute a major cost factor. This is evident where a high-cost raw material is used, for instance, gold, or where a very large volume of a raw material is used, such as in the generation of electricity. A reduction in these costs may be achieved through seeking new sources of supply or by a redesign of the product which would seek to reduce the volume of material. It might also be possible to use an alternative material.

Cost reductions may be achieved in divisions and departments. Regular targets are those activities which do not have much impact on turnover in the short term. Depending on the nature of the business, these would include market research, public relations, advertising, education and training, and research and development. It may be necessary in the short term to reduce the size of these functions but their absence in the longer term is likely to lead to yet another crisis.

The final area for cost reductions is general overheads. This would include staff functions such as computing and head office staff. Also, the fringe benefits offered by the company could be reduced. This would include company cars, free or subsidized meals, sports and recreation facilities, pensions and holidays. At a more mundane level, heating, lighting, stationery, typing facilities can also be scrutinized.

Asset-reduction Strategies

The impact of asset-reduction strategies is not often apparent in the short term. The policy likely to have the biggest impact in this category is the divestment of a division or complete operating unit to another company as an operating business. In many crisis situations, loss-making subsidiaries are sold and this has the immediate effect of stemming the outflow of funds and of raising revenue. However, the disadvantages are that the subsidiaries are unlikely to be sold at anything more than asset value and, considering the losses, perhaps at considerably less than asset value.

Selling a successful division has the merit of securing a higher price and thus increasing the current cash flow, but in the longer term, the associated profits will be lost and the sold company might have provided a basis for long-term recovery.

An alternative asset-reduction strategy is a rationalization of existing facilities, closing one plant and transferring the manufacture of the products of that company to another business in the group. The unused facilities can then be sold in parts. The sale of specific assets, including land or buildings, can be effected without complete closure of a plant and offers another means of reducing assets and obtaining cash.

Another means of reducing assets is to sell some or all of the assets to a finance company and lease them back. This would only be possible if the assets were not being used as collateral for some form of borrowing.

The foregoing discussion is primarily concerned with fixed assets, but working capital offers another area for consideration. A reduction in stocks and work-in-progress will reduce the asset base and release cash. Reducing debtors and increasing the length of time to pay creditors also reduces assets and releases cash, but creditors are unlikely to allow this to continue if the crisis in the company is apparent to those outside. In some cases, the creditors may be 'locked-in' because to insist on payment may push the company into liquidation, which would probably result in only a small percentage of the debt being repaid.

Revenue-generating Strategies

Revenue-generating strategies are usually those which take the longest time to have a significant impact on profitability, because most frequently this is the part of the business which is the crux of the problem and will be most difficult to turn around and also because expenditure is often required before extra income is generated.

Some immediate effects may result from a sharp impetus to the selling function, which could be achieved through increasing incentives to salesmen or small alterations to the product. However a longer-term marketing strategy may have no discernible effect in the short term, as the process requires time for information-gathering, decision-making, the manufacture of new or modified products, and the preparation and implementation of a sales campaign.

12.5　MANAGEMENT SUMMARY AND CHECKLIST

1　Symptoms of decline

- Financial: falling profitability, falling dividends, increased debt, decreasing liquidity.
- Marketing: falling sales.

2　Causes of decline

- Poor management: autocratic CEO with weak top management.
- Finance: poor financial control.
- Marketing: no operationalization of the marketing (as opposed to selling) concept.

- Production/operations: high cost structure.
- Acquisition policy: no comprehensive strategy to the process of acquisition.
- Big projects: failure of a project which constituted a large proportion of the firm.
- Declining industry sales: failure to acknowledge decline or adapt to the situation.
- Industry structure changes: changes which put the business at a significant disadvantage.
- Other environmental variables: technological, social, political, economic.

3 Feasibility of recovery determined by:

- Favourable or unfavourable industry characteristics.
- Relative strengths and weaknesses of the business.

4 Strategies for recovery

- Organizational changes
- Finance and financial strategies
- Cost reduction
- Asset reduction
- Revenue generation

Note: Not all symptoms and causes of decline are evident in all cases and sometimes some of these features may exist but the firm may not experience declining profitability. Similarly, feasibility of recovery and strategies for recovery may not be in evidence in all cases.

NOTES

1   E. I. Altman, *Corporate Bankruptcy in America* (Heath, 1971). W. H. Beaver, 'Financial Ratios as Predictors of Failure', *Journal of Accounting Research*, Supplement to Vol. 4 (1966) pp.71–111. R. Taffler and H. Tisshaw, 'Going Going Gone – 4 Factors which Predict', *Accountancy* (March 1977).
2   R. A. Eisenbeis, 'Pitfalls in the Application of Discriminant Analysis in Business Finance and Economics', *Journal of Finance*, 32, no. 3 (1977), pp. 875–900.
3   J. Argenti, *Corporate Collapse – The Causes and Symptoms* (McGraw-Hill, New York, 1976).
4   K. Harrigan, *Strategies for Declining Businesses* (Lexington Books, Lexington, Mass., 1980).
5   Stuart Slatter, *Corporate Recovery* (Penguin, Harmondsworth, 1984).

FURTHER READING

A fuller understanding of the issues in this chapter can be obtained by reference to the following books:

1   J. Argenti, *Corporate Collapse – The Causes and Symptoms* (McGraw-Hill, New York, 1976).
2   D. B. Bibeault, *Corporate Turnaround: How Managers Turn Losers into Winners* (McGraw-Hill, New York, 1984).
3   Peter H. Grinyer, David G. Mayes and Peter McKiernan, *Sharpbenders: The Secrets of Unleashing Corporate Potential* (Blackwell, Oxford, 1988).
4   K. Harrigan, *Strategies for Declining Businesses* (Lexington Books, Lexington, Mass., 1980).
5   S. Slatter, *Corporate Recovery* (Penguin, Harmondsworth, 1984).

PART IV
Strategic Choice

13 Entry and Exit Strategies

Acquisition—Cooperative Strategies—Divestment:
Reasons and Methods—Divestment: Management
Buy-outs—Tactical Strategies—Management Summary
and Checklist

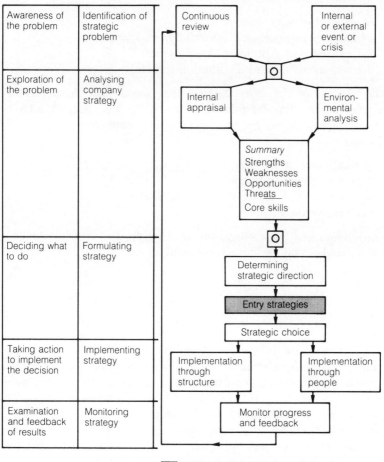

FIGURE 13.1 The strategic decision-making process

The process for determining possible future options for the company was outlined in part III. That process was concerned principally with the ends not the means. The means, the decision to make (internal development) or buy (acquisition) or indeed to sell (divestment), are the focus of this chapter. An investigation of the means by which the ends might be achieved is an essential precursor to the next chapter which draws the process to a conclusion by an evaluation of the available options and the choice of a given strategy. It is certain that not all desired options can be attained, the principal obstacles being time or cost or both.

As the means are a critical factor in determining whether a desired option can be achieved, it will be useful to examine some general barriers to entry and exit. There exists a large range of entry barriers but perhaps the four most significant are:

- economies of scale;
- a patent or technological information or know-how;
- the existence of significant brand names;
- the non-availability of distribution outlets.

Some aspects of the entry barriers may also result in substantial exit barriers. In particular, the following four factors have been found to be the most frequent reasons for the reluctance of companies to exit from an industry:

- non-differentiable assets;
- capital intensive industry;
- age and level of depreciation of the assets;
- poor realizable price.

Additionally, loss leaders or a loss-making product which is an essential part of a range may create exit problems.

13.1 ACQUISITION

There are basically three ways of entering new markets or offering new products: acquisition, internal development or cooperative ventures. Co-operative ventures (joint ventures, minority interest, licensing, franchising, selling agents) are a hybrid of the other two entry strategies in that, rather than complete self-sufficiency or total acquisition, there is a sharing of the process which starts at product development and ends with sales to customers. It follows, therefore, that the advantages and disadvantages of internal development and acquisition are also applicable to joint ventures. A summary of the reasons for adopting these alternative entry strategies is outlined in table 13.1. Of the factors listed, timing and cost are usually the critical variables.

TABLE 13.1   Internal development versus acquisition

Internal development	Acquisition
is pursued when	is pursued when
• the product is in the early stages of the product life-cycle (PLC)	• the product is in the maturity or decline stages of the PLC
• the new products or markets are close to the existing portfolio	• the company has little knowledge of the products or markets it wishes to develop
• there is sufficient time to develop internally	• earliest entry is desirable
• there are no suitable acquisitions	• there are few internal development skills within the company
• there is no production capacity in the industry	• there is production capacity in the industry
• costs need to be spread over time	• costs do not need to be spread over time

The overall cost of development will be a consideration, but may be cheaper by either means according to the specific factors apparent in the particular project under consideration

This chapter will consider, in turn, acquisitions, cooperative ventures and specific tactical strategies for new market entry. The strategy of acquisition is the penetration of a new market or the extension of the product range through the purchase of a firm in that business, thus instantly acquiring the requisite skills and resources, although they may not currently be operating to satisfactory performance standards. At this point it may be useful to examine whether there is any significant difference between a 'merger' and a 'takeover'. There appears to be a growing tendency to use the former term rather than the latter, possibly because it seems less hostile, yet the fact is that in many instances it is a takeover which is taking place between a 'bidding firm' and a 'victim'. There does not seem to be a consensus of definition, and as far as the City is concerned they are considered to be equally applicable.

The issues surrounding mergers will be discussed in sections relating to the time sequence of an acquisition: before, during and after.

Before the Bid

It will be useful to start with the key question: why do companies seek to merge? The question is all the more pertinent as research substantially supports the view that merger is usually both more risky and more expensive than internal growth.

The motives for merging are usefully summarized in figure 13.2 and are divided into defensive and offensive reasons. It should be emphasized that this is only a summary and that each item is capable of considerable expansion. For instance 'Gains in financial strength' could emerge as a result of tax advantages, gearing changes, better utilization of assets (turnaround situations) and so on. Also the diagram does not indicate the importance and effect of timing, not only with respect to the date on which the bid is made, but also in that assets and skills can be acquired more quickly than is likely through internal development.

The next question is: how do companies merge? What is the process which needs to be followed in order to maximize the likelihood of success? There are basically five steps:

1   Have clear objectives for the merger

The reasons for the merger need to be made explicit in terms of the financial and product market portfolio effects on the acquiring company. These objectives will result from the internal and external (SWOT) analysis and the projected future financial aims and objectives of the business as a whole. It should be appreciated at this early stage that no target company is likely to satisfy the specific criteria in every respect, and that it is possible that a choice will have to be made from a range of possible companies each offering satisfaction with respect to different criteria. For example, a company satisfying most of the criteria may be well managed and successful and therefore more expensive than a company satisfying fewer criteria but at a lower price.

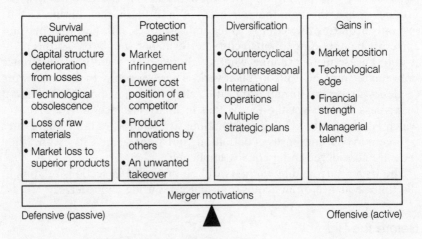

FIGURE 13.2   Motivations to merge
Source: F. T. Haner, *Business Policy Planning and Strategy*, (Winthrop, Cambridge, Mass., 1976). Reprinted with permission.

2   Be satisfied that major objectives are achievable

It follows that, as there is rarely an 'ideal' target, it is important to focus on the key features of the objectives to ensure that they will be satisfied. The basic financial return will need to be achieved and this will be a function of the price paid and the future cash flows received after acquisition. If the expected future cash flows need to be greater than those at present, the means for increasing the flows and the time period over which they can be expected must be carefully analysed. Most acquisitions have some product-market portfolio aims and, if these will only be met in part, the implications should be be considered and ways of completing the fulfilment of the aims need to be outlined. Unless the firm is to be closed and the assets sold, some evaluation has to be made of the target company management and its ability to meet the desired aims and objectives which are being planned by the acquirer.

3   Prepare strategy to include top price and offer package

A strategy is a complete game plan and contains contingency plans – if the target companies react in *this* way, then we, the acquiring company, will take *that* action. It is not possible to outline a comprehensive plan including all contingencies in an introductory text, but it is intended to outline the key features which should enable the reader to devise a game plan appropriate to any given situation. In general, valuation of a company is made on the basis of its assets and the ability of those assets to generate earnings. There are firms where the net assets per share comfortably exceed the market price of the share because its earnings are not at a satisfactory level. In cases where this situation is known to those outside the company, there could be several bidders who believe that they can use the assets more profitably.

Invariably the question will be: what premium over the existing share price should be bid? In such situations the experience of the merchant banks becomes invaluable and often both sides take on advisers. In the case of Fitch Lovell the shares had underperformed the food sector by 18 per cent in the year before acquisition. The bid by Booker valued Fitch at approximately 300p; this was a 40 per cent premium on the share price before the bid was announced. The price offered was 14 times current earnings against an average market p/e of 10–12, thus Booker were expecting to be able to make better use of the assets than the existing management team.

The purchase price offered is made up of:

(a) cash per share; (b) 'X' shares of the acquirer for every 'Y' shares of the target; (c) a combination of (a) and (b). In the case of publicly quoted companies, we have generally available financial information such as share price, EPS, p/e ratio, and so on. Also, when a bid is made, the usual form is for the proposed 'victim' to forecast its future earnings and other performance factors (especially if in the second half of its year) and/or revalue its assets (that is, update valuations of its property holdings, etc.).

However, of crucial important is the comparison of the p/e ratios. If that of the bidding firm is lower than that of the 'victim', then by purchasing via shares it would dilute its earnings per share (not desirable), and it is, therefore, pressed into paying cash. Thus we can see the importance to quoted companies of maintaining a high p/e ratio; first, defensively in keeping predators away and, secondly, to be used offensively if bidding for a firm with a lower p/e ratio. The effect of the p/e ratio is discussed in more detail in chapter 8.

4 Purchase plan

The following outline maps out one possible route by which a company may be acquired. It may be regarded as 'typical' or 'idealized' and is based upon procedures and rules for the London Stock Exchange.

Step 1   The would-be buyer collects information on its target. Normally this is done in secret – which often means there is a heavy reliance on published data. A maximum and an initial offer price are thereby fixed for the target. Where possible, information regarding the identity of the target's principal shareholders should also be gathered.

Step 2   The next step is optional. A stake may be acquired in the target company – it can be used as a springboard from which to launch a full bid. As long as the size of the stake does not exceed 3 per cent of the target company's issued share capital, the purchase can be kept secret (Sections 24–7 Companies Act 1985).

Step 3   When all is prepared (offer document, finance etc.), the buyer approaches the board of the target company and asks it to approve the bid. In order to help assure the success of the bid, it is normal for the buyer to offer a significant premium over and above the current trading price of the target's shares, in cash, buyer's shares or a mixture of the two.

Step 4   If the directors of the target company approve the bid they will then send the offer out to their shareholders asking for their acceptance.

Step 5   Initially, the bid is conditional. More than 50 per cent of the target company's shares must be offered to the bidder by the shareholders, or the would-be buyer can withdraw. Once this threshold has been exceeded the offer is declared unconditional – thereafter shareholders of the target who have agreed to sell their shares may not then withdraw.

Step 6   Various time limits have been fixed by which the various phases of the bid must be completed. Normally the offer must be open for acceptance by the target company's shareholders for at least 21 days after the offer was posted.

Step 7   If the buyer gains acceptance for 90 per cent of the target's shares within four months of making its offer, it can arrange a compulsory purchase of the remainder (Section 209 Companies Act 1948).

This very simple outline assumes that the Department of Trade and Industry, the Bank of England and the target's board of directors all approve the bid.

5   Responsibility for the purchase

It is important to be able to identify who is responsible for the final decision to acquire another company. This has the advantage of ensuring that the bid is the focus of at least one person, and does not allow the decision to be the outcome of a committee from which no one may take the individual responsibility for seeking to ensure its success. This person may be the chief executive, the chief of corporate planning or (more likely in a multidivisional company) a divisional managing director. The responsible person needs to be afforded all necessary resources, which would be part of the plan successfully to facilitate implementation.

In concluding the pre-bid stage it is important to note some ways in which a company can deter likely predators.

- Enhance share price through good shareholder relations, public relations, contact with the financial press.
- Make long-term contracts with directors and suppliers.
- Avoid financial attractions such as spare debt capacity, excessive cash and use sale and leaseback to avoid asset strippers.

During the Bid

The 'purchase plan' was outlined previously and the comments which describe the strategy as a complete game plan are again relevant, particularly in view of the various defensive tactics which the victim might pursue, such as:

1   Revaluation of assets and profits forecast

Some companies do not revalue assets regularly and thus a bid may be made on a wholly unrealistic valuation. During the BTR bid for Dunlop it was shown that the offer price was considerably below a price based on a revaluation of the assets. Likewise, it is possible to provide a profit forecast which indicates a considerable improvement on current performance. However, this defence is subject to the Takeover Code rules which ensure as far as possible that the figures are realistic both for revaluation and for revising the profits forecast.

2   Rubbishing the bid

Almost all companies use this technique. This defence is often used in conjunction with a revaluation and rejects the bid in the most sarcastic terms, concentrating on future earnings, lack of synergy and industrial logic, or by taking the offensive and attacking the competence of the bidding company and its management.

3   Publicity campaigns

A recent defence used to influence shareholders has been an extended publicity campaign highlighting strengths and pinpointing opposition weaknesses. Several campaigns are considered to have cost considerably in excess of £1 million.

4   White Knights

In order to escape the unwanted attentions of a would-be buyer, the target company can submit to another 'more sympathetic' company, a White Knight. This strategy is pursued when the target company management accept, at least implicitly, that their own stewardship has led to the current situation. It may not be considered a defence in that the company does lose its identity; however, it is a tactic that a bidder may have to deal with.

5   New share issue

The City Code has now effectively stopped the use of this tactic in the UK but it could be possible elsewhere in the world.

5   Monopolies and Mergers Commission

As a defence tactic the victim would need to persuade the MMC that the merger was against 'the public interest', possibly by creating a company with such a large market share as to create a monopoly and thereby reduce consumer choice and increase prices. This tactic if successful can be an absolute defence or, even if unsuccessful, it can gain time for the target company to adopt other defensive measures. Lonrho and House of Fraser is a good example.

7   Going private

Management buy-outs are becoming increasingly common, but their use as a defence technique is very unusual. It is possible that this is seen as management acting in their own interest. However, research in the USA (where the practice is more common) indicated that shareholders received an average 56 per cent above the market price.[1] The UK example is Haden (a lift and air-conditioning contractor) rebuffing the unwanted attentions of Trafalgar House (May 1985).

8   Friendly third parties

The target company persuades a third party to become a shareholder. By doing this the third party 'mops up' shares on the market which might otherwise be sold or pledged to the unwanted bidder. Also, it acts as a blocking stake in that it may, with the directors' shareholding, constitute more than the 50 per cent of the shares required by the bidder to gain control. It also helps to maintain the target company share price. Tootal escaped from the Australian company Entrad with the help of the intervention of the bankers J. Rothschild and Co. who built up a stake in this manner.

9   Selling the crown jewels

Disposing of major assets (the crown jewels) during a takeover is now extremely difficult as the City Code forbids it. However, in the USA it is still possible.

10   Acquire new assets

This strategy seeks to increase the size or improve the profitability in order to reduce the attractiveness of the victim. While Waddington were being pursued by BPCC, they acquired the Business Forms division of Vickers which made them larger, stronger and improved the balance between divisions.

11   Porcupine defences

These are a range of strategies, currently used in the USA but not in the UK, whereby the victim makes adjustments to the equivalent of the memorandum and articles of association.

12   Golden parachute

This technique is the payment of bonuses to management in the event of a successful bid. This again is used in the the USA but not presently in the UK.

After the Bid

The post-acquisition phase is often the most crucial, and consequently management needs to re-focus attention on the reasons for the takeover and to take appropriate action to ensure that the expected benefits materialize. Some of the major problems experienced are outlined below.

1   Management problems

Integrating the acquired company into the acquiring firm has to be achieved through people. New systems, plans and strategies can only be implemented if the necessary skills are available in the acquired business. The simplistic view that all management can be removed and replaced by hiring a more competent group of staff is usually unrealistic. It is immediately obvious that this will take time and assumes that the needed characteristics are evident and that those with such characteristics will want to join the firm.

Morale and damaging internal political conflicts (see chapter 15) can affect the size of and rate at which expected benefits are realized. If morale is low, care needs to be taken to ensure it does not fall even further, and this can be done by making major decisions quickly in order that the fears of change can be set aside.

If part of the reason for the acquisition was to obtain the services of key members of the management team of the acquired company, then early discussions may be necessary to ensure that they do not leave.

These issues may seem trivial or appear to have obvious solutions, but it is often the case that the success or failure of a merger results from the way in which these problems are resolved.

2   Competition

It is possible that the takeover will change the competitive environment in the market (see chapter 6) and that such changes may provoke a reaction from other firms in the same business. Changes in the competitive environment may significantly affect the original objectives and expected benefits of the merger. If the changes were likely to have an adverse effect, management might choose to ignore the situation as they were committed to the original objectives. This is not a wise course of action. In some cases, renewed effort and some changes to plan may bring results, but if the evidence is that the merger cannot now bring the desired benefits, it may be better to abort the project at minimum cost. The fear of failure and bad publicity cause some managements to pursue a course which, because of a reluctance to admit a mistake, leads to even bigger problems.

3   Finance

Management problems and changes in the competitive environment are not the only reasons why many of the strategic advantages are often illusory. Unless it is an *agreed* bid and the acquirer can investigate the business from inside, there are many unknown factors. If the benefits are significantly less than anticipated, it is important to accept the situation and adopt appropriate rectification measures. For instance, any over-payment should be funded to reserves and actually written off or provision made for it to be written off.

13.2 COOPERATIVE STRATEGIES

The 'do-it-yourself' (internal development) approach to new products or markets and the purchase (acquisition) of a company operating in new products or markets are points at each end of a continuum. Between these points there are ways of developing new products or markets which arise from inputs from different businesses. One business may supply the product, another the marketing skills. Two companies with a need for a particular raw material may decide that they will start a business and share output and profits. This section is concerned with describing some of the major forms of these cooperative strategies.

Joint Ventures

A joint venture is a business which is jointly owned by two or more businesses and usually manufactures a product or provides a service which is of importance to each of the parent businesses. It may provide raw material for their production or an outlet for their product or waste products. In a joint venture the shares owned by each participating firm may not be equal, so that each might have a major, equal or minor stake. This would depend not only on the finance invested but also on any technological input. For instance, the supplier of a raw material which has very limited uses may wish to ensure a purchasing commitment from the buying firms and seek to do this by a stake in the new company. The supplier would be bringing not only finance but also a considerably greater share of technological knowledge to the process and so would be expected to have the greatest share. Joint ventures are also popular between businesses manufacturing the same product but operating in a new market.

Temporary Collaboration

In the construction industry temporary collaboration between two firms is often necessary where the size of a civil engineering project is greatly beyond the resources of any one business. Such collaboration may also take place in circumstances where the good or service is on a 'one-off' basis. In the service industries, temporary collaboration may be necessary in management consultancy or auditing, although in recent years many firms in these businesses have joined together on a permanent basis in order to cope with large-scale requirements.

Selling Agents

A simple form of cooperation is the appointment of agents to sell the products of the business. The advantage is that an extensive sales coverage network can be established cheaply as salaries and expenses of the salesmen are not part of the costs. However, the major disadvantage is that there is no control over the selling function, that is, the quality of sales staff and their commitment to the product, especially if they are selling a range of products. Selling agents are most regularly used by UK companies to develop overseas markets where the establishment of an agency will not only be inexpensive but will have the advantage of better knowledge of local conditions.

Licensing

Licensing is an arrangement whereby a business, often in an overseas market, is permitted to manufacture or sell a product which is often protected by patent. This most frequently occurs in technologically based industries such as chemicals and machinery manufacture. The advantage is that greater exploitation of the product is achieved in a given time scale. The major disadvantage is that some profit may be lost, as compared with the production by the business holding the patent.

Franchising

In recent years franchising has increased in importance as a cooperative strategy. Franchising is similar to licensing and is an agreement to permit another business to undertake part of the business process, normally either production or marketing. The problem with all cooperative strategies, but particularly with licensing and franchising, is that if quality, reliability and service are not up to standard, the reputation of the originating firm can be damaged. As a result, those companies with a strong product that are using cooperative strategies as a means of development allocate significant funds to training and development of their chosen collaborators in order to maximize sales and minimize potential problems.

13.3 DIVESTMENT: REASONS AND METHODS

During the past two decades the business strategy of many firms has been focused on growth by diversification and by acquisition. It follows that the product-market portfolios of many large companies contain businesses which are small and peripheral to the main activities of the firm as a whole.

With the accent on growth, little attention has been paid to the subject of divestment: the exit from businesses no longer wanted in the portfolio. However, for a variety of reasons the latter part of the 1980s has seen many companies exit from businesses for a variety of reasons and in several different ways.

The period of growth was fuelled by the desire to grow big and thus, it was hoped, to enable the company to control a larger part of its operating environment than if it was small. It is also noteworthy that directors' salaries were related to the size of company turnover and not profit. However, the advent of corporate raiders such as T. Boone Pickens in the US and Hanson and BTR in the UK have made diversified companies address the fundamental question of synergy. Do two businesses joined together into one corporation add up to more than the sum of the parts? If so, all is well and good. If not, then let them be put asunder.

There are several reasons both offensive and defensive which might cause a company to consider divestment. Such divestments have been of small, non-core parts of the organization, but occasionally as with BTR in the 1960s (tyre manufacture) it has been a major activity of the firm.

Outlined below are some offensive and defensive reasons for divestment.

Offensive reasons

- in re-focusing the total business, this part is no longer required, even though it may meet profitability standards;
- to raise cash;
- to improve ROI;
- family company with no future family succession.

Defensive reasons

- does not and cannot be made to meet profitability standards;
- avoid acquisition (BAT is an example which sold businesses in order to avoid the unwanted attention of a predator);
- sell this part of the business in order to avoid bankruptcy;
- avoid risk: future prospects or expansion are at a level of risk which the company does not wish to embrace;
- management control of such a diverse business has become too difficult.

The process of divestment can pose some very difficult problems. It is possible that the business for disposal may be highly profitable and attractive to several buyers. However, the opposite is more often the case and as such the price obtained for such assets may be well below that paid for them as a result of a contested takeover in the past. Wright and Coyne suggest six different ways of exiting from a business.[2] In fact, not all of the divestment options involve complete loss of ownership and/or control:

- franchising
- contracting-out
- sell-off
- management/leveraged buy-out
- spin-off or demerger
- asset swap/strategic trade.

For some types of business franchising may afford the best divestment opportunity, particularly where local service or small-scale manufacturing facilities would be desirable. Contracting-out is similar to franchising, but differs in that having sold the business the vendor requires the business to supply a quantity of the goods or services at a price usually for a specified time period. This gives the business guaranteed sales and the parent an assured source of supply.

The most widely described form of divestment is the sell-off. In this way the parent sells the business to another business and severs all connection. Another form of divestment is the leveraged or management buy-out which, given its recent rise as a form of exit, is afforded a separate section (13.4). With large corporate predators around demergers are beginning to appear as a form of divestment; Courtaulds, for example, is creating two companies: one for its textile business and one for its chemical business. Finally, an occasional means of divestment is the asset swap. In this case little money transfers hands but a 'match' has to be found before this means of exit can be pursued.

13.4 DIVESTMENT: MANAGEMENT BUY-OUTS

A separate section on management buy-outs (MBOs) has been included for two reasons. First, they provide a new and increasingly used means for divestment. Secondly, unlike the other forms of divestment outlined by Wright and Coyne, the parties involved are different in terms of number and by nature. In an MBO there are at least three major interested parties as compared to two for other divestment situations. There are the vendors, the buyers and the venture capital providers. The vendors' role is not significantly different from other situations. However, the buyer is a group of managers who are usually going to put, what will be for them, a substantial equity stake into the new business. Other means of divestment are not usually of any major consequence to capital providers. In some cases the buyer may use internal funds and where capital is required there is a proven track record which reduces the need for detailed in-depth analysis. Also, divestments are often relatively small in terms of buyer and seller total assets. In order to explore the role of MBOs in the divestment process factors which need to be considered by each of the parties are outlined below.

Vendors

From the vendors' viewpoint the MBO often offers a more rapid and flexible approach to exit. It is not necessary to search for a buyer and all involved are conversant with the facts of the company, its value and associated risks.

It is often more satisfactory from a public relations viewpoint to sell to the managers and it certainly pre-empts the problem of 'walking' managers; that is, managers who decide to leave the company once the vendors' intention to divest becomes known. In some cases the knowledge, skills and expertise of the managers is such that were they to leave the value of the company would be substantially diminished. It also avoids the bad publicity and associated costs should closure be the only alternative.

It is more likely that, if desired, the vendor will be able to maintain a stake in the business as the buy-out team are usually looking for capital suppliers so that, provided it is a minority stake, this will usually be acceptable to both vendor and buyer. The vendor is also more likely to accept a discount on independent valuation of the company, either for personal reasons, or for financial reasons such as walking managers.

MBO Team

The MBO team may be motivated by the prospect of continued employment, enhanced job satisfaction or increased financial reward. These may all be viewed as positive attractions: however, there is considerably increased financial risk as the team members borrow money and use their own property as security.

A major advantage for the team as compared to other buyers is that they are in a much better position to determine the expected future cash flows of the business. They may be able to see opportunities in the new situation which are not available to them in the current organization with its policies, procedures and structures. The buy-out team may be in a stronger bargaining position if their knowledge of the business is such that their resignations would cause the value of the firm to fall. This issue, together with the fact that the managers have a bid, may well dissuade would-be purchasers to come forward.

At this early stage of MBOs as a form of divestment, research is limited in volume and conclusions need to be carefully drawn as the long-term results are not yet in existence. With this caveat some results should be noted. MBOs are less likely to fail over their first two years than new start-ups. Many MBOs are followed by redundancies but also by subsequent net recruitment in real jobs and several experience cash-flow problems. This latter point is not unexpected in view of the highly geared nature of the capital structure of many of these new businesses. A further finding is that relationships with employees, customers and suppliers all improve subsequent to the formation of the new company.

Venture Capital Suppliers

Potentially successful MBOs are much sought after by capital suppliers as the failure rate over the first two years is 1 in 8 compared with over 50 per cent for new start-ups. In comparison with new start-ups, MBOs offer a history of operating, an existing management team and an ability to predict with more certainty the likely future potential of the business.

The venture capital is primarily concerned with the financial package. The balance between the various forms of debt and equity needs to be organized such that it does not imperil the financial viability of the company. On the other hand, the risk and return have to be balanced in order that the capital provider will be prepared to invest. It is not the purpose of this chapter to discuss valuation but this is also clearly a key issue in determining the attractiveness of the investment.

13.5   TACTICAL STRATEGIES

In searching for strategic alternatives it is possible to identify one or more products or markets which would provide the means to achieve given company objectives. However, if this task is completed in isolation it is possible that problems will occur. If it is not possible to enter the target markets or develop the new products because of the dominance of companies already in the market and their likely reaction to a new entrant, then the entrant company may find that instead of enhancing profitability, the attempted entry has been extremely costly. The ability and means to enter a new market or develop a new product are therefore crucial in successful diversification moves.

The overall strategies used to develop new products or markets have been discussed previously in this chapter. This section is concerned with tactical strategies.

There are potentially many strategies which can be used as a basis to gain entry, but this section will contain four major variants. If these variants do not describe a given circumstance, the reader is encouraged to map the situation in a similar manner in order to establish the nature of competition and possible entry strategies.

Confrontation

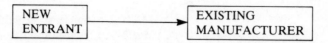

In this strategy the new entrant seeks a 'head-on' confrontation with the existing competition. There are not many circumstances in which head-on confrontation is likely to be successful. Evidence of the existence of one or two key features of the competitive situation would need to be present before considering the head-on strategy. First, if the new entrant has a significantly distinctive competitive advantage, through price, product features and so on. Wilkinson Sword had such an advantage when they entered the razor-blade market which was dominated by Gillette. Secondly, a head-on confrontation may be possible if the existing suppliers have become complacent and are unlikely to respond; such was the case with Smiths in the potato-crisp market. Also, some businesses may be unable to respond with sufficient speed because of a rapid change in the competitive situation. An example would be building societies. Long-term contracts, government and other regulations, patents and market dominance are factors which can create inflexibility and complacency and permit a head-on confrontation to succeed.

Satellite

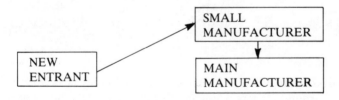

In the satellite strategy a company enters by means of manufacturing and selling the product or a very similar product on a small scale in order to gain production and marketing experience, and then it launches a full-scale attack on the main market. If the satellites are segments, then it may be necessary to occupy several or all before the attack. This is known as encirclement. The difference between this strategy and the confrontation strategy is that in the satellite strategy the entrant to the major product gains prior experience of product and market, whereas in the head-on strategy the firm enters the market with much less, if any, experience.

Guerrilla

In the guerrilla strategy it is difficult to gain experience by manufacturing or supplying on a small scale, maybe because small and large scale require fundamentally different skills, and thus a segment of the whole will need to be the initial focus. Apart from the inability to gain sufficient production and marketing experience, opposition from the major manufacturer is likely to be greater, even though it may only be a small part of the total business. If no opposition was the expected response, the direct confrontation might be more appropriate. In the chemical industry a large number of small manufacturers have developed businesses based on speciality chemicals. Also, Marks and Spencer retail clothing for all age groups, but are now under competition in various segments from chains such as Next.

By-pass

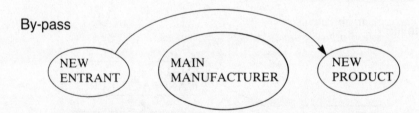

The by-pass strategy is used when the current industry is overtaken by a substitute product. There are many examples: for instance, the introduction by electronics firms of digital watches, computer companies manufacturing word processors and thus by-passing the typewriter industry, and frozen-food manufacturers by-passing the canned and dried food business.

13.6 MANAGEMENT SUMMARY AND CHECKLIST

The future shape and direction of the company will be significantly determined by the ability to enter and exit from businesses at a time and cost which are attractive in relation to the objectives. There are many entry and exit barriers and some of those most regularly influencing decisions are:

Entry barriers

- economies of scale
- a patent or technological information or know-how
- existence of significant brand names
- non-availability of distribution outlets.

Exit barriers

- non-differentiable assets
- capital-intensive industry
- age and level of depreciation of the assets
- poor realizable price.

There are three key means of entry:

- *internal development* using existing company resources;
- *acquisition* of a firm currently operating in the new business area;
- *cooperative strategies* involving cooperation with other companies.

1   Advantages of internal development and acquisition

See table 13.1

2   Considerations before the bid

- have clear objectives;
- be satisfied major objectives are achievable;
- prepare a strategy to include top price and offer package;
- prepare a purchase plan.

3   Considerations during the bid

In the plan, the bidding company must be prepared for the following defensive tactics:

- revaluation of assets and profits forecast
- rubbishing the bid
- publicity campaign
- White Knights
- new share issue
- Monopolies and Mergers Commission
- going private
- friendly third parties
- selling the crown jewels
- acquire new assets
- porcupine defences
- golden parachute

4   Considerations after the bid has been completed

This phase of the acquisition process is often the most crucial in determining whether the takeover will be successful or not. Key areas for attention are:

- management problems: need to focus on and strive for original objectives
- competition: reactions of competitors
- financial problems: financial data and control systems and funding.

5   Cooperative strategies

The more widely used forms of cooperation are:

- joint ventures: joint ownership with other companies
- temporary collaboration: joining together for a single project
- selling agents: agents to sell goods
- licensing: license other firms to make the product
- franchising: agreement to permit other firms to undertake part of the process of manufacture and distribution.

6   Reasons for divestment

Offensive reasons

- in re-focusing the total business, this part is no longer required, even though it may meet profitability standards;
- to raise cash;
- to improve ROI;
- family company with no future family succession.

Defensive reasons

- does not and cannot be made to meet profitability standards;
- avoid acquisition;
- sell this part of the business in order to avoid bankruptcy;
- avoid risk: future prospects or expansion are at a level of risk which the company does not wish to embrace;
- management control of such a diverse business has become too difficult.

7   Methods of divesting

- franchising
- contracting-out
- sell-off

- management/leveraged buy-out
- spin-off or demerger
- asset swap/strategic trade

8 Key actors in a management buy-out (MBO)

- vendor
- MBO team
- venture capital supplier.

9 Tactical strategies

The tactics for entry need to be considered as a game plan. Four tactical entry methods are:

- confrontation: a head-on confrontation
- satellite: begin by selling on a small scale or regionally
- guerrilla: attack a segment
- by-pass: produce a product which makes the existing product redundant or places it at a significant disadvantage.

NOTES

1 M. C. Jensen, 'Takeovers, Folklore and Science', *Harvard Business Review*, 62 (Nov–Dec 1984), pp. 109–20.
2 M. Wright and J. Coyne 'Management Buy-outs in Britain – A Monograph', *Long Range Planning*, 20, no. 4, pp. 38–49.

14 Deciding on Future Strategy

Introduction–Critical Criteria—Strategic Fit—Deciding Among Strategic Options—Management Summary and Checklist

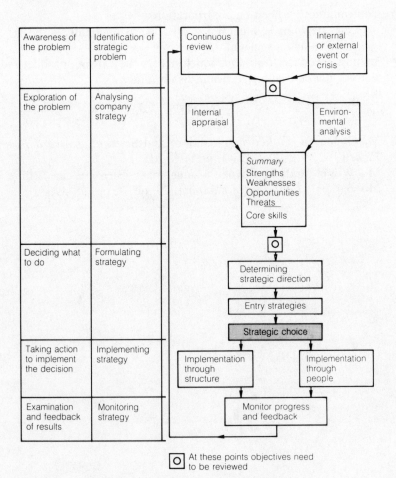

FIGURE 14.1   The strategic decision-making process

14.1   INTRODUCTION

The part of the strategic decision-making process outlined in part III will produce a range of strategies which may provide a means for meeting the long-term financial goals of the company. It is the purpose of this chapter to outline the means by which each of these possibilities may be evaluated in detail. In this evaluation there are three key stages (figure 14.2).

First, an assessment against key criteria. These criteria are of such fundamental importance that the failure of a potential project to satisfy any one of them immediately removes it from the list of possible future options.

Secondly, the detailed evaluation of all projects which have satisfied the critical criteria. Finally, the actual choice of options. At this stage it is necessary to assess the likely opposition to a given strategic move and to consider the impact of timing on such a move.

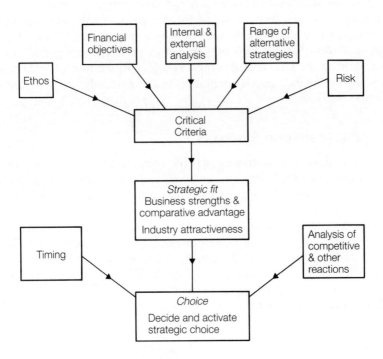

FIGURE 14.2   Process of strategic choice

14.2 CRITICAL CRITERIA

Criteria which are critical to strategic choices concerning the future will vary from company to company and over time, and will emerge from different parts of the strategy analysis. What follows is a brief description of the way in which critical criteria arise, together with some examples. It is not intended to be a comprehensive checklist.

Financial Objectives

The financial objectives of the company provide the first, and arguably the most important, set of critical criteria. The company will set ROCE and EPS targets and will have DCF and Payback standards which will work towards the overall targets. Thus, a project which does not meet the minimum standard would be rejected unless there was some highly significant mitigating circumstance.

Internal and External Analysis

The internal and external analysis would have provided an outline of the major strengths and weaknesses of the company and the key threats and opportunities in the environment in which it operates. Thus, if a key weakness was that the company was too vertically integrated, or too dependent on the UK economy, then a project for the future would have to avoid increasing the vertical integration and to have substantial potential in overseas markets.

Range of Alternative Strategies

The range of alternative strategies is the result of the process described in the previous two chapters. The outcome is a list of different products or markets which the company might enter and an outline of the possible means of entry.

However, some companies have blocks on certain strategies and so some future avenues will have remained unexamined. For many years Thomas Tilling had a policy of no divestment. Hanson has a policy of avoiding high-tech industries. So company policy can be constrained by critical criteria in the area of strategic alternatives, and hence no future options will be considered which contravene these rules.

Ethos

The word ethos is used here to convey ethical, cultural and organizational standards which may not be considered elsewhere. In ethical terms the firm might decide not to do business with certain political regimes (South Africa, Communist countries) or not to manufacture products which are harmful or cause a health hazard (smoking). A company may decide not to do business in countries in which the culture is significantly different from the culture of the country of origin of the firm. Organizationally, there may be policies with respect to pay, training, redundancy, unionization which would be difficult to implement in the target market, and therefore the project would be rejected.

Risk

All companies have an implicit or explicit risk profile, that is, there are limits to the expected amount of risk that the top management of a company are prepared to accept. In many companies the project which provides a very high return but is associated with a very high degree of risk would be rejected in favour of a project with a lower return at lower risk. In the risk scenario the company is concerned with the extent of the shortfall from the expected result and the probability of each shortfall estimate occurring. In this regard, the use of sensitivity analysis in order to make reasoned estimates of risk is essential.

14.3   STRATEGIC FIT

There are a large number of techniques available to aid the process of selecting from alternative courses of action. A comprehensive review of these options is provided by Hofer and Schendel[1] but it is intended here to concentrate on a limited range of those more widely used. It should also be noted that, as all are based on specific assumptions, the reader is encouraged to use them as a general guide to which there will be exceptions. A more comprehensive critique of the techniques is available from a series of articles in *The Financial Times* (beginning 12 November 1981) and elsewhere.[2]

Boston Consulting Group (BCG) Matrix

The BCG framework is based on two variables, the rate of growth of the market and the relative market share (see figure 14.3). Some of the major assumptions on which the matrix is based are that:

- the market can be defined;
- profitability and market share are positively related;
- there are no barriers to entry or exit in the market concerned;
- the stage of industry maturity can be defined;

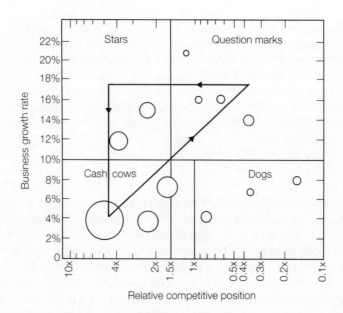

FIGURE 14.3   BCG business portfolio matrix
Relative market share is the ratio of the firm's size to that of its largest competitor.
Source: B. Hedley, 'Strategy and the "Business Portfolio"', *Long Range Planning* (February 1977), p. 12. Reprinted by permission, Pergamon Journals Ltd.

- the market is still in the positive growth stage;
- two dimensions are sufficient to describe the competitive situation.

It may seem, given these assumptions, that there is unlikely to be any market which satisfies all these criteria. However, conceptually the model helps an understanding of many markets, identifies the likely direction of cash flows, and provides a basis for a more balanced product-market portfolio.

To use the matrix, a firm would determine the values of each dimension for each of its products and when placed in the matrix this would provide an overview of the company portfolio. It would indicate whether the parts of the business were concentrated in one area. The theory suggests that portfolios should be reasonably balanced among Stars, Cash cows and Question marks and that this is the desired direction for continued success and profitability. A company may develop a product in a high-growth market which initially has a low market share (Question mark). The company should plan to increase the market share and thus move the product into the Star category. While the product remains a Star it is unlikely to release cash as, given that the market is still growing rapidly, the cash generated and maybe more, will be required for new plant to satisfy the increases in demand. As the market growth rate slows down, less cash is required for reinvestment and thus the product automatically becomes a Cash cow, the cash being released rather than used for reinvestment. As the growth slows even further, the theory enables revitalization to the Question mark stage and so the cycle begins again. Dogs are low market-share products in a declining industry, and so the firm should exit from these businesses unless there is a special reason for not doing so.

If there are too many Stars, a cash crisis may result, if too many Cash cows, future profitability may be in jeopardy, and too many Question marks may affect current profitability.

Again, it needs to be stressed that the model needs to be used as a general tool for analysis, to which there will be exceptions.

General Electric (GE) Business Screen

The GE matrix has two dimensions, industry attractiveness and competitive position. However, on inspection, these two variables are capable of including all the factors which are likely to affect the profitability of a company. Thus, while the BCG is criticized for over-simplification, the GE matrix may be regarded as over-complicated. As with the BCG, it is important to accept that the model is useful conceptually and will enable more appropriate strategies to be adopted than if no framework is used to evaluate the portfolio of the firm.

A version of the matrix is shown in figure 14.4 and, after some explanation of the model in general, the means of determining industry attractiveness and competitive position will be discussed.

The top left-hand sector of the matrix (high industry attractiveness, strong competitive position) is the most desirable segment and the lower right-hand segment (low industry attractiveness, weak competitive position) is the least desirable. However, companies can operate in most segments successfully provided they adopt an appropriate strategy and timing schedule. The number of factors incorporated in the two dimensions means that successful operation in any one sector is contingent upon certain features. Such contingencies are elaborated in more detailed texts.[3]

Dimensions of Industry Attractiveness

The eleven key features of all industries and markets that are important in evaluating industry attractiveness are summarized below. The issues involved in understanding industries and markets were discussed in detail in chapter 6, and consequently only a brief discussion of their main features will be outlined here.

Size   What size is the market? Is it sufficiently large to enable objectives to be met?

Business strengths

		Strong	Average	Weak
Industry attractiveness	High	• Grow • Seek dominance • Maximize investment	• Evaluate potential for leadership via segmentation • Identify weaknesses • Build strengths	• Specialize • Seek niches • Consider acquisitions
	Medium	• Identify growth segments • Invest strongly • Maintain position elsewhere	• Identify growth segments • Specialize • Invest selectively	• Specialize • Seek niches • Consider exit
	Low	• Maintain overall position • Seek cash flow • Invest at maintenance levels	• Prune lines • Minimize investment • Position to divest	• Trust leader's statesmanship • Attack on competitor's cash generators • Time exit and divest

FIGURE 14.4　Strategic moves within the GE matrix

Source: C. W. Hofer and M. J. Davoust, *Successful Strategic Management* (A. T. Kearney Inc., 1977) p. 52. Copyright © 1977 by C. W. Hofer and M. J. Davoust, reproduced by permission.

Growth rate　What is the growth rate of the market?

Position on the PLC　In what phase of the PLC is this product/market?

Production differentiation　Is the product 'commodity-like' or is it differentiable?

Profitability　What is the profitability of other companies in this industry?

Cyclicality　What is the extent of long-term or seasonal cyclicality in the industry?

Structure of the industry　What is the structure of this industry? – oligopolistic, dominant firm, etc. What is the nature and extent of concentration?

Barriers to entry　What is the nature and extent of any barriers to entry in this industry?

Level of technology　What is the level of technology in the industry? What level of R&D would be required?

Supplier characteristics   Are there special features which need to be considered of any raw material, bought out part or services?

Buyer characteristics   Are there any special features which need to be considered of the customers for the products in this market?

When seeking to establish industry attractiveness it is important to do so in respect of the entrant firm, that is, attractiveness is not an abstract issue but, as in human terms, is 'in the eye of the beholder'. An industry which may be attractive to one company will be unattractive to another. Also, the attractiveness of an industry will vary from time to time.

Another important feature in the process is the actual means of selection. There is a considerable danger of developing analysis paralysis at this stage and there is a need to focus on the key issues, both positive and negative, when deciding on the relative merit of different product or market options.

Finally, a point which links with the next section. No situation is static and this makes description difficult. It is important therefore to monitor current, and to forecast likely future, changes taking place in the market in order to reach the best calculated conclusion.

Dimensions of Business Strengths

The evaluation of the business strengths of the company was the subject of the internal analysis in chapter 7. Therefore, it is not intended to reiterate the issues in detail at this point.

The key areas in which the company will have core skills and key resources are:

- management
- finance
- marketing
- people and organization
- production
- research and development.

As with industry attractiveness, business strengths need to be considered in the context of the industry under consideration. What might be a strength in one industry may be a weakness in another. Also, as before, an appreciation should be made of the changes likely to take place in the market and their impact on the business.

Evaluation of Business Strengths against Industry Attractiveness

At this stage of the choice process, strategic fit (see figure 14.2), some possible future products have been 'screened out' in the critical criteria phase. For instance, a company which was too dependent on the UK economy would remove from the list of potential future products or markets any which provided opportunities only in the UK.

The process of seeking new opportunities was discussed briefly in chapter 7. What appears in this section is the detailed analysis which is necessary to investigate all opportunities thoroughly. There are basically two approaches to the analysis, quantitative and qualitative. Each requires the preparation of a list of the key features of all products or markets to be investigated under four functional headings: markets and marketing, finance, production and personnel, as outlined in table 14.1.

The quantitative approach adopts a weighting and a rating for each feature and multiplies the two figures to result in a score. The scores for all features are then aggregated to produce a total score for that particular product or market opportunity. This can then be compared with other potential future product or market opportunities. As with most rigid systems, the outcome needs to be treated with caution as both the weighting and the rating are subjective figures. The overall total for each opportunity should, therefore, be used not as an absolute mechanism to decide between alternatives, but rather as a starting point for discussion. For purposes of calculation the weighting is the level of importance to the company of a given feature and the rating is the extent to which the product or market being investigated satisfies that feature.

A similar but qualitative approach would list the same criteria on the left-hand side and have two columns headed strengths and weaknesses. Thus, for each criterion, a qualitative assessment is made of its relative position in the given situation. Deciding between alternatives, this technique is based on the relative strengths and weaknesses of each project.

These two attempts at measurement are merely formalizing the thought processes which will be necessary in seeking to select among future portfolio options.

Strategic Fit and the Product Life-cycle (PLC)

Although the PLC is either implicit or explicit in the BCG and GE models, it is not the major focus of either. There is now considerable evidence to suggest that the life-cycle has an influence, not only on the functional activities of the company (figure 14.5) but also on its corporate strategy. Specifically, even if a company is a market leader throughout the cycle, different strategies will be necessary. The implications of the position of the product on the PLC are discussed in chapters 6 and 7.

The two dimensions to the matrix shown in figure 14.6 are business strengths and stages in the PLC. At the development stage, usually few companies are able to gain substantial market share and the advent of new competitors with improved products often results in a large number of

TABLE 14.1   Evaluating alternatives

	Weighting	Rating	Score
Markets and Marketing			
Size	3		
Growth	2		
Position on product life-cycle	3		
Concentration	2		
Cyclicality	2		
Export potential	1		
Relationship to existing markets	2		
Financial factors			
DCF/rate of return/payback estimates	3		
Cash required	2		
Increase to overall profitability	3		
Value added (per man, per £1 capital)	1		
Production factors			
Knowledge of production process	2		
Utilization of surplus facilities	2		
Availability of raw materials and supplies	1		
Personnel			
Availability of factory workers	1		
Availability of management and technical staff	1		
Strength and militancy of union	2		

The weighting for each variable will remain the same for each product assessment. The rating however will change as shown in the example for instance with respect to market growth.

Variable	Measure	Weighting	Rating	Score
Market growth		2		
	Over 10% per annum		5	
	7½% to 10%		4	
	5% to 7½%		3	
	2½% to 5%		2	
	0 to 2½%		1	
	Below 0		0	

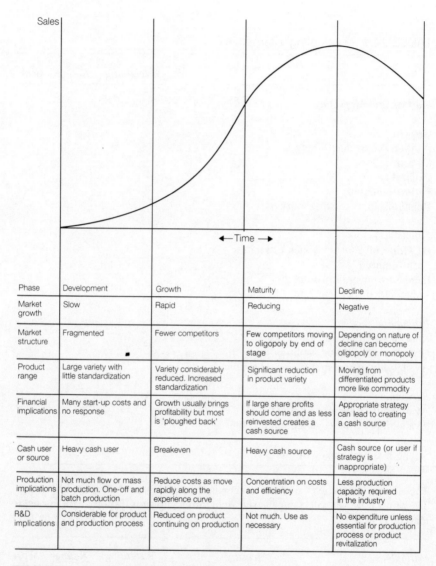

FIGURE 14.5　Life-cycle effects on strategy

Phase	Development	Growth	Maturity	Decline
Market growth	Slow	Rapid	Reducing	Negative
Market structure	Fragmented	Fewer competitors	Few competitors moving to oligopoly by end of stage	Depending on nature of decline can become oligopoly or monopoly
Product range	Large variety with little standardization	Variety considerably reduced. Increased standardization	Significant reduction in product variety	Moving from differentiated products more like commodity
Financial implications	Many start-up costs and no response	Growth usually brings profitability but most is 'ploughed back'	If large share profits should come and as less reinvested creates a cash source	Appropriate strategy can lead to creating a cash source
Cash user or source	Heavy cash user	Breakeven	Heavy cash source	Cash source (or user if strategy is inappropriate)
Production implications	Not much flow or mass production. One-off and batch production	Reduce costs as move rapidly along the experience curve	Concentration on costs and efficiency	Less production capacity required in the industry
R&D implications	Considerable for product and production process	Reduced on product continuing on production	Not much. Use as necessary	No expenditure unless essential for production process or product revitalization

suppliers with very varied product offerings. In this situation the company which is high in business strengths must concentrate on increasing market share which can usually be achieved through marketing alone. Those with lower advantages must also seek to increase market share, but may choose to do so not only through marketing but also by the more risky means of acquisition. The risk at this stage is because the future direction of the market – in terms of product features and so on – may render redundant

Stage in the PLC	Business strengths		
	High	Average	Low
Development	*Share increasing primarily through marketing*	*Share increasing through marketing or merging*	*Share increasing Turnaround Quit*
Growth	*Maintain or increase share primarily through marketing*	*Increase share through marketing or merging*	*Increase share Turnaround Quit*
Maturity	*Maintain or increase share primarily through marketing or some acquisitions* *Efficiency strategies*	*Increase share through merging Shrink selectively*	*Quit*
Decline	*Maintain or increase share* *Selective acquisitions*	*Shrink selectively Quit*	*Quit*

FIGURE 14.6   Typical strategies through the life-cycle

the products of the acquired companies. For very low strengths the strategies are either to seek to turn the company round or to leave the industry.

During the growth stage the focus for the companies with high business strengths should be to maintain and, if possible, increase market share – again, this is likely to be achieved primarily through marketing. For those in the 'average' category, increasing share now becomes imperative if the company is going to gain maximum benefits in subsequent stages of the PLC. Marketing will still be the main means to reach this goal, but mergers become an increasing possibility. For those with low business strengths, this is most likely to be the last chance to gain future benefits. Therefore, since the strategies of maintaining share and concentration on efficiency are likely to be expensive, the three most likely strategies remain increasing share, turnaround, and leaving the industry.

In the maturity stage the market gets more concentrated and product differentiation reduces significantly. For the high business strength companies it is important at this stage to maintain market share and reap the benefits of the experience curve, thus focusing on cost reduction. For those with average strengths the only way to increase share is through merger; or as an alternative strategy it can seek to withdraw from the market gradually by blocking new investment and generally 'running down' the business. It is thus said to shrink selectively. Those who find themselves in the low strengths category should quit the industry, seeking to minimize losses.

Once demand starts to fall the cohesive state of the oligopolistic market gets disturbed. Maintaining market share means lower sales and profit, excess capacity and redundancy. In these circumstances, it is likely that competitive action, often a price-war, will follow in order to maintain sales levels which means, in a declining market, gaining market share. What follows will depend on a large number of factors and is well documented by Harrigan.[4] However, in this situation the most likely steps are for the stronger companies to increase market share, probably through a series of acquisitions which will require partial or total asset reductions. For those with average strengths, profitability is likely to be low and so shrinking selectively or quitting are the most appropriate options.

If the market is segmented and the major companies do not operate successfully in some of the small segments, then this will afford specific opportunities for smaller manufacturers at several stages and positions in the process.

In summary, strategic fit is concerned to evaluate the appropriateness of possible future strategic options with the current and projected strengths of the company.

14.4   DECIDING AMONG STRATEGIC OPTIONS

From the strategic fit analysis a final list of acceptable projects will emerge and action will be taken to implement the strategies. However, several factors may result in a further stage in the process. For example, there may not be sufficient cash available to proceed with them all, or, if the effect would be to double the size of the company in a short period, this may put unacceptable strains on top management.

Also, it is important to review what are the likely reactions to a given course of action. All those who have a stake in the company are likely to be affected by strategic decisions. Such groups may include:

- national government
- local government
- customers
- competitors
- employees and trade unions
- shareholders and money lenders
- suppliers.

If any of these groups perceive themselves to be significantly affected in an adverse way, it is probable that in time they will take action to counteract the unsatisfactory aspects of the policy, and this in turn may wholly or partially frustrate the strategy so that the desired goals can no longer be achieved.

A final and often neglected feature of selecting a strategy is that of timing. There are two aspects of time which are relevant: first, the point in time in which a strategy will be initiated and, secondly, the time that it will take for the full cash outflows and revenues to be realized. The importance of timing is perhaps more fully appreciated by referring back to the military analogy, although many examples exist in the field of business strategy. In a military campaign, the plans are coordinated in such a way that if an action occurs too early or too late, the whole plan can fail. Good timing can be attributed to luck, but good planning emphasizes the importance of doing the right thing (strategy) at the right time. The size of the project, the risk and the timing are closely interwoven.

14.5 MANAGEMENT SUMMARY AND CHECKLIST

1   Initial screening consists of reducing the list of possible new opportunities on the basis of some critical criteria:
- the range of alternative strategies developed from the SWOT analysis;
- key features of the SWOT analysis with respect to future products and markets;
- financial objectives of the company;
- risk profile of the company;
- ethical and other non-quantitative policies.

2   The suitability of any particular product market option is determined by using either or both of the following:
- BCG matrix
- GE matrix

3   Key dimensions of industry attractiveness are:
- market size
- market growth
- position on the product life-cycle
- product differentiation
- profitability
- cyclicality of profits
- structure of the industry
- barriers to entry
- level of technology
- supplier characteristics
- buyer characteristics

4   Dimensions of business strength in these areas:
- management
- finance
- marketing
- people and organization
- production
- R&D

5   Effect of the product life-cycle in determining strategy.

6   Strategic choice – the analysis has been completed and it only remains to choose among the options, considering both the timing and the likely reactions of competitors or other parties affected by the decision.

NOTES

1   C. W. Hofer and D. Schendel, *Strategy Formulation: Analytical Concepts* (West Publishing Co, St Paul, Minnesota, 1978).
2   Douglas Brownlie, 'Strategic Marketing Concepts and Models', *Journal of Marketing Management*, 1, no. 2 (1985).
3   M. E. Porter, *Competitive Strategy* and *Competitive Advantage* (Free Press, Glencoe, 1980 and 1985); K. R. Harrigan, *Strategies for Declining Businesses* (Lexington Books, Lexington, Mass., 1980).
4   Harrigan, *Strategies for Declining Businesses*, chapter 2.

PART V
Implementing Company
Strategy

15 Implementing Strategy

Introduction—Behaviour and Politics—Leadership—
Organizational Design—Planning—Controlling
Strategy—Management Summary and Checklist

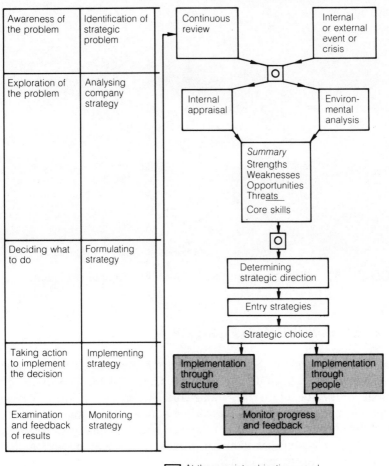

FIGURE 15.1   The strategic decision-making process

15.1   INTRODUCTION

The key features of the implementation process and its role and position in
the overall planning process are outlined in figure 15.2.

The strategy is determined by the process described in previous chapters
and this now has to be implemented by specified personnel in the
company. Two separate features of implementation through people will be
discussed, first behaviour and politics, and then leadership style and roles.
Also certain features of the structure and systems of the firm can facilitate
or detract from the successful implementation of policy. These features are
the organizational structure, the planning function, and the control systems
adopted, and are discussed in turn.

FIGURE 15.2   The role of implementation in strategic decisions

15.2   BEHAVIOUR AND POLITICS

In order to implement the chosen strategy successfully it is important to
understand the behaviour and political features which result from the
actions of personnel in the framework within which they work. As
corporate decisions concern the business as a whole, they are likely to
affect the life and job prospects of large numbers of employees and as such,
most strategic actions are likely to provoke a reaction among employees
which may be favourable or not.

In order to examine the internal behaviour of the company, it is useful to
think of the political process running in parallel with the planning system.

While there might be some short-term misalignment, the two processes must operate in harmony over the longer term. If 'politics' in this context describes how people interact in a given system, it cannot, as is sometimes the case, be regarded as something to be avoided. It exists and is the means by which decisions are implemented. In essence, politics is concerned with power and its use, and consequently with the resolution of conflict.

The power developed by a person in an organization may arise from a variety of sources. The formal position in the company structure will provide power in terms of superiors, subordinates and peers. The access to and control over information or a particular skill or knowledge may afford opportunities for the acquisition and use of power. Finally, power may be gained by rapid and direct access to persons with power together with the ability to influence their decisions.

The successful implementation of strategy will require cooperation across a variety of personnel and departments within the company. In most organizations this informal interdepartmental cooperation reduces the need for formal procedures, and hastens implementation as well as improving morale. However, there can be some debilitating effects of political action, as when personal or departmental goals deflect the organization from its long-term objectives.

Resistance to change was discussed by Schon.[1] He stated that organizations are conservative, that is, they do not readily accept change. The argument went further in stating that organizations exhibit *dynamic* conservatism and that that is not only a desire to stay as they are. In addition, they fight to maintain the status quo, and to do this five different strategies could be adopted.

- Ignore and take no action to implement the change.
- Launch a counter-attack to get the decision reversed or modified.
- Contain the change within a specified area.
- Isolate the change by not integrating it into the organization.
- Respond by the least change capable of neutralizing or meeting the undesirable intrusion.

The result of any of these actions will be a failure fully to implement the strategic decision or a failure to do so in the desired time. Such actions are a major source of conflict in the implementation process.

A means for resolving conflict is critical in the implementation of *strategic* decisions, as delay or failure to meet objectives may have serious consequences because either is likely to affect the business as a whole rather than one department, product or division. The first step is to accept that conflict *will* occur and that consequently some process is necessary to resolve the conflict.

Conflict can arise from a variety of sources: competition for scarce resources, conflict as a result of some feature of the organizational structure, or a difference in personal values, aims or management style. Conflict is often regarded as destructive and to be avoided because of the emotional stress and tendency to deflect attention from the ultimate goals. However, some conflict situations can have constructive outcomes in those circumstances where it challenges complacency or stimulates alternative ideas and actions.

It is not possible to provide a process for resolving conflict which would be applicable in a wide range of situations and thus it is appropriate, having done the analysis, to encourage the implementer to develop appropriate resolution mechanisms.

15.3   LEADERSHIP

The successful implementation of any strategy will be dependent on the quality of the leadership. In this section the job of the leader will be examined, together with leadership styles and roles appropriate for different circumstances.

The work done by managers can be considered under three main activities: planning, organizing and leadership. Within each, there is a subset of tasks which go to make up the whole. While these are shown separately in table 15.1, the inter-relationships are extensive.

The planning role requires investigating skills such as problem definition and information-gathering, processing and presentation. For evaluating a situation it is necessary to be in possession of relevant knowledge and theory. However comprehensive the analysis of a problem, there are always unknown factors; and thus decision-making is the balancing of all the known facts against the risks associated with alternative courses of action. The final step in the planning process is the need to set up procedures to monitor and feed back information relating the progress achieved towards the given objectives. This needs to be done with the realization that the procedures introduced will affect the way people behave.

TABLE 15.1   Managerial tasks

Planning	Organizing	Leading
Investigating	Organizing the structure	Supervising
Evaluating	Staffing	Giving orders
Decision-making	Communicating	Motivating
Controlling	Coordinating	
	Negotiating	
	Representing	

The output from the planning function will be decisions to take action. To ensure that desired goals are achieved, it is necessary to organize the resources of the institution to meet these ends. The first step in organizing is to develop an appropriate structure. Once achieved, there is a need to provide staff to fulfil the structure. Once in post, there is then a need to ensure that the structure is operating efficiently which will require communication, coordination and negotiation skills. From time to time it will be necessary for the leader to represent the interests of the company on some outside body.

The actual task of leading involves the supervision of activities, the giving of orders and the ability to motivate subordinates in such a manner as to meet the objectives outlined by the planning function.

The management style of the senior management of an organization is essentially concerned with the degree of participation and the role of planning. Some companies are led by autocrats who make all the major policy decisions, while in others there is greater participation at senior management level and a desire to reach a consensus on major issues. The extent of the effect of planning on major issues would again vary widely. Some companies would only make major decisions as a result of the planning process, others would use the information as part of the decision-making process. Finally, many companies, including some with departments which have titles such as 'corporate planning', make major strategic decisions with little or no reference to the planning function. The style adopted by senior management will have a fundamental effect on subordinates and how they manage, and consequently on the success of the organization as a whole.

An alternative way of looking at leadership is to study the roles required of the CEO or senior management. Much research, particularly by Mintzberg, has been concentrated in this field.[2] In essence, there are considered to be two major managerial roles: informational and decision-making. Shapira and Dunbar consider the informational element to include such roles as figurehead, liaison, disseminator and spokesman, and the decision-making element to include leader, monitor, entrepreneur, negotiator and allocator.[3]

15.4   ORGANIZATIONAL DESIGN

Organizational design has a key role in the implementation of strategic plans. Generally, the design of an organization should be a function of the chosen strategy; indeed, failure to adjust the organization to new strategic tasks can seriously undermine the chosen strategy. It could be argued that the success of any strategy depends upon organizational effectiveness.

Organizational structure can contribute to the achievement of strategic objectives in a number of respects:

Structure | in terms of implementation by defining tasks and roles and allocating people and resources to them
Operating system | by indicating what is expected of people in roles via operating procedures and reward systems
Decision mechanisms | by facilitating communication, decision-making and reporting systems
Organizational health | the effect upon morale and motivation, the elimination of conflict and the nature of responsiveness to external threats and opportunities.

In reality, organizations are rarely designed; they grow and acquire a structure, but there is a constant responsibility for senior managers to question the appropriateness of the structure of their organization. Basically, senior managers have to reconcile or balance the conflicting pressures:

1   Pressures of standardization, control, predictability, efficiency and uniformity.
2   Pressures of uniqueness, diversity, segmentation, new technologies, flexibility and responsiveness.

While there is no best organizational form, managers have to take into account a number of factors when adapting the organization, as can be seen in figure 15.3.

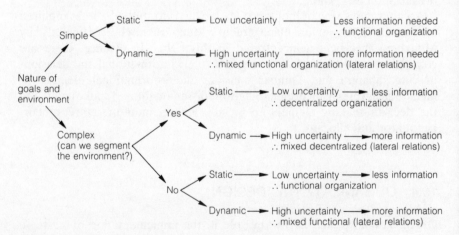

FIGURE 15.3   Organizational design decision tree
Source: R. Duncan, 'Characteristics of Organisational Environments and Perceived Environmental Uncertainty', *Administrative Science Quarterly*, 17 (1972), p. 313.

15.5   PLANNING

Systematic comprehensive corporate planning used to determine the corporate future of a company is not widely in evidence in industrial organizations.

When corporate planning became a subject for study in the mid 1960s, many books and articles failed to discuss implementation, somehow believing that, having gone through the rational decision-making process, the recommendations would in some mysterious way become reality. While implementation is now an accepted component of the strategic decision-making model, many businesses have failed to integrate their corporate planning system effectively into the company policy-making process. The result is a diminution of the *value* of the corporate planning activity. It is sadly a fact that whereas many departments termed 'marketing' are doing no more than selling, so many corporate planning departments are doing no more than budgeting. Steiner outlined ten reasons which caused planning systems to fail.[4]

1 Failure to develop throughout the company an understanding of what strategic planning really is, how it is done in the company and the degree of commitment of top management to doing it well.
2 Failure to accept and balance inter-relationships among intuition, judgement, managerial values and the formality of the planning system.
3 Failure to encourage managers to do effective strategic planning by basing performance appraisal and rewards solely on short-range performance measures.
4 Failure to tailor the strategic planning system to the unique characteristics of the company and its management.
5 Failure of top management to spend sufficient time on the strategic planning process, with the result that the process becomes discredited among other managers and staff members.
6 Failure to modify the strategic planning system as conditions within the company change.
7 Failure properly to mesh the process of management and strategic planning from the highest levels of management and planning through tactical planning and its complete implementation.
8 Failure to keep the planning system simple and to monitor constantly the cost–benefit balance.
9 Failure to secure within the company a climate for strategic planning that is necessary for its success.
10 Failure to balance and appropriately link the major elements of the strategic planning and implementation process.

While each of the causes of failure is important, the role, commitment and time allocated by the chief executive officer (CEO) is critical to the successful implementation of corporate planning. All that follows in this chapter, indeed the complete contents of this book, are an irrelevance unless the CEO is committed to planning as the way by which the company is to be managed. Bad planning becomes bureaucratic and restrictive, and can slow decision-making, and so although planning may be the style chosen for managing company affairs it needs to be flexible and alert to changes in the assumption on which it is based. A rigid adherence to plans written on tablets of stone and handed down from generation to generation is not likely to lead to the best future for the company.

The major value in planning is in the process of thinking through the business/environment interface, and as such it needs to be based on real dialogue between the board and planners on the one hand and the operating companies on the other.

15.6   CONTROLLING STRATEGY

As can be seen from chapter 14, implementation involves key questions about who is going to implement the plan, what they are going to do and how they are going to do what is required. Closely allied to any implementation strategy is the notion of control. The essence of strategic management is that senior managers are in control of the organization such that when performance becomes 'off-track' they know why. This necessitates the creation of systems and procedures which ensure that managers know what is required of them in a given time frame and that they are given appropriate feedback on their action and the general state of areas they are responsible for. Clearly, different managers in a hierarchy are responsible for differing parts of the chosen strategy as illustrated in figure 15.4.

Styles of Control

Recently, interest has been shown in how companies plan and control their strategies, particularly in diversified companies. Goold and Campbell[5] identified three types of company:

Strategic planning companies: head office actively involved. Long-term planning at the top.

Financial control companies: strong financial control. Targets for subsidiaries tend to have a short-term profit orientation.

Strategic control companies: a mixture of the above. Head office assists. Delegation and ownership of targets to subsidiaries.

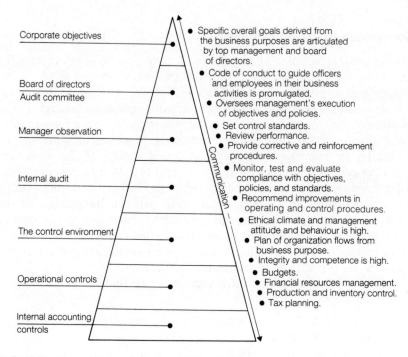

FIGURE 15.4   Hierarchy of control activities
Source: Adapted from A. L. MacKay, 'Management Control in a Changing Environment', *Financial Executive*, March 1979, p. 25.

No one style is the 'best' and all have been successful, but the style chosen is often a function of diversity and chosen strategic directions.

Planning and Control

It has been argued by Anthony that planning and control are a single process.[6] There is too a set of problems when they are divorced; for example, mismatches between responsibility and authority or one-half assuming primacy over the other when, for example, the control system runs the planning system which tends to foreshorten managers' time horizons. Planning in this regard tends to have a shorter time horizon than, say, the strategic plan. In many organizations this would be an annual process, but as such should be congruent with the long-term plan. Given that the overall annual plan will be created to achieve predetermined targets, for example EPS, ROCE, the plan needs to be broken down such that specific responsibilities can be assigned. Such a disaggregation process will result in specific programme areas which may reflect, say, differing functions in an organization, or specific SBUs, but the end result is a series of specific programmes designed to achieve corporate objectives.

Control and the Budget System

The budgetary control system is the most usual process employed for the control of the corporate plan. Budgets are essentially the result of the disaggregation process described above, where programme areas are costed, resulting in specific financial targets for individual managers. The involvement of managers in the budget creation process often forms part of the resolution of the top-down and bottom-up processes of planning.

Clearly, an important consideration is the design of the budgetary control system as it affects important concepts of authority, responsibility, accountability, coordination and consistency. Further, while not part of this chapter, there is a strong relationship between budgeting and the behaviour of managers. For example, managers who decide to save money by cutting services in one part of an organization can have a detrimental effect on others. Further, budgets can have a behavioural context in that they can and are used as instruments of motivation.

The establishment of a control system using budgets necessitates a number of steps:

- decide what to measure
- create performance standards
- collect data and measure actual performance
- compare standards against actual
- take corrective action exceptionally.

While the above may appear rather obvious, considerable care needs to be taken when making decisions about the implementation of these steps.

Deciding what to measure necessitates the manager having to come to important conclusions about the critical success factors in his or her part of the business. Managers have to decide which key factors influence the basis of the information system. The creation of performance standards often leads to the need to coordinate with other functions as well as providing the opportunity to motivate managers as budget-holders. The collection and transmission of data concerning corporate and departmental performance is expensive but has the potential to offer real advantage to a company. The use of such data for evaluation purposes is important, for it allows managers the opportunity to assess the degree of control they have over elements of their budgets. In many instances, organizations have to set parameters around what constitutes off-track performance and the amount of discretion managers have to change the strategy or tactics as a consequence. Too many changes can destroy the system's integrity and it could be argued that a policy of no changes can be sustained as long as it is within agreed tolerances and further that the reasons for disparate performance are well known.

Patterns and Procedures

Many organizations proliferate operating manuals, standard procedure manuals, safety procedures, pricing systems, recruitment procedures and so on. In a real sense these are often manifestations of the tasks involved throughout an organization in order to accomplish a given strategy. Such sets of tasks also act as guides to the 'doing' part of the strategic process. In some industries they are required by law. In many they add to the organization's competitiveness, for example, Total Quality Management (TQM), and in others they are vital, for example in franchising, where the company finds it difficult to exercise frequent control. They are useful devices provided they contain a sequenced set of tasks designed to accomplish an activity or target. They are, however, at the mercy of strategic change and often they tend to be left unaltered for a considerable time until they become positive barriers to the accomplishment of a chosen strategy, then they are updated and made more relevant. They are particularly important for developing new staff and for organizing daily work.

Problems in Strategic Control

Short-term orientation

A distinct danger with budget systems is that they can turn managers into short-term thinkers because of the perceived necessity to get it right every month. There has to be a clear distinction created within the organization between the long and short term. This often results in organizations developing sets of long- and short-term measures as in table 15.2.

Goal displacement

This is when strategies become goals. For example, a sales team which erects a goal of sales maximization may achieve the goal at the expense of profits.

Expectations

Phrases such as 'I thought it was what you would want' are often evidence of sub-objectives and consequent strategies and tactics not being fully explained.

Sub-optimization

This occurs when managers do what they think is right for them or their function despite the plan. The ability to control this type of behaviour may depend upon the sanctions!

TABLE 15.2 Long- and short-term measures

	Short term	*Long term*
Markets and customers	Sales volume Sales value New customers	Growth in sales Loyalty of customers Ability to sustain prices
Factor market	Cost of supplies Stock levels Delivery/ availability	Relationships with suppliers Growth rates in short-term measures
Production	Produced cost Reject and scrap rates	Cost savings Plant layout Facilities plans
Finance	EPS Market value ROCE	Stock-market image ROCE

15.7 MANAGEMENT SUMMARY AND CHECKLIST

1 Behaviour and politics

- Are there political factors which are deflecting attention and effort from strategic goals?
- Is the conflict constructive or destructive?
- Are organizational problems causing the conflict?

2 Leadership

- Who are the actual leaders in this company?
- Is there evidence that they have the right characteristics to achieve the strategic objectives?

3 Organizational structure

- What is the nature of the environment with respect to the rate of change?
- What is the level of complexity of the operational activities of the business?
- Is the organizational structure appropriate for these key dimensions?

4 Planning

- What is the commitment of the CEO to corporate planning?
  Does the head of corporate planning report to the CEO?
  Is the long-term future of the company the result of work done by the corporate planning department?
- Is the planning system comprehensive, flexible and capable of rapid adaptation to incorporate the results of an unforeseen threat or opportunity? *OR* is it partial, bureaucratic, inflexible and incapable of responding to new information?

5 Control

- Are the standards defined those which will monitor progress towards the given objectives?
- Are the measurements quantified and achievable?
- Are the evaluation and action procedures adequate?
- Are there features of the control system which will have undesirable consequences?

NOTES

1 D. Schon, *Beyond the Stable State* (Penguin, Harmondsworth, 1969).
2 Henry Mintzberg, *The Nature of Managerial Work* (Harper & Row, New York, 1973).
3 Zur Shapira and Roger L. M. Dunbar, 'Testing Mintzberg's Managerial Roles Classification using an In Basket Simulation', *Journal of Applied Psychology* (Feb, 1980).
4 G. A. Steiner, *Pitfalls in Comprehensive Long Range Planning* (The Planning Executives Institute, Oxford, Ohio, 1972).
5 M. Goold and A. Campbell, *Strategies and Styles* (Blackwell, Oxford, 1988).
6 R. N. Anthony, *Planning and Control Systems: A framework for analysis* (Harvard University Press, 1965).

Glossary of Terms

Where appropriate, regularly used abbreviations are shown in brackets.

Accumulated depreciation The amount of depreciation which has accumulated over time and which is written off a fixed asset.

Acid test Another name for liquidity (see liquid ratio).

Assets Tangible or intangible items possessed by the firm which can be expressed in monetary terms and which will benefit the firm's operation, e.g. plant and equipment, stocks, goodwill, cash.

Asset turnover Ratio of sales to net tangible assets.

Authorized share capital The limit of share capital which a company can issue at any given time. Also called nominal share capital or registered share capital.

Average collection period The average time over which a company collects monies owing from its debtors.

$$\frac{\text{debtors} \times 365 \text{ days.}}{\text{sales}}$$

Bonus shares Shares issued gratis to existing shareholders, sometimes referred to as a scrip or a capitalization issue.

Book value The valuation of an asset as recorded in the balance sheet. Usually represents acquisition cost less accumulated depreciation.

Business planning Involves the process of establishing objectives and the development and implementation of strategy, extending down to the development of sales forecasts, establishment of budgets, anticipation of needs for capital and facilities and equipment.

'Cash Cows' Low-growth products that usually generate more cash than is required to maintain market share. Generally regarded as the foundation of the firm.

Concentration ratio   The percentage of the industry output manufactured by the 'N' biggest firms in that industry. Substitute '5' for N and this is called the 'Five firm concentration ratio'.

Convertible loan stock   Stock holding which may be converted by the holder at some future date into ordinary shares.

Cost of capital   The cost to a company's ordinary shareholders of issuing shares or debentures, of retaining profits, or of other sources of funds.

Creditors   Money owed by a company resulting from say, the purchase of materials.

Cross-Elasticity of demand   The relationship between the price of one good and the demand for another.

Put more formally: $$\frac{\text{Percentage change in sales volume of Firm A}}{\text{Percentage change in price of Firm B}}$$

If positive then products are substitutes; if negative, then they are complements. Useful in defining who the competition is.

Cumulative preference shares   Preference shares which have a payment priority on the arrears of their dividend over dividend on the ordinary shares. Arrears must be stated in the balance sheet.

Current assets   Assets which are either cash or will be expected to become so within a year from the date of the last balance sheet. For example, stocks, debtors.

Current liabilities   Liabilities which, it is assumed, will have been paid within one year from the date of the balance sheet (e.g. creditors, current taxation).

Current ratio   Ratio of current assets to current liabilities.

Debentures   Loans which may be secured on the assets of the company.

Debtors   Monies owed to the company. e.g. customers' outstanding debts. Normally shown in the balance sheet net of provision for debts unlikely to be recovered.

Deferred taxation   Tax which is due at a date beyond one year from the date of the balance sheet.

Depreciation   Expense recording the using up of fixed assets through operations. Usually measured by allocating the historical cost less disposable value of the asset on a straight-line or reducing-balance basis.

Discounted cash flow (DCF)   The present value of future income and payment; i.e. their value, taking into account the anticipated gap between receipts and payments.

Diversification　A strategy by which the firm's growth objectives are achieved by adding products or services to the existing lines. Concentric diversification takes place when the products added are similar to existing types, from a production, marketing channels, customers or technology point of view. Conglomerate diversification is growth into areas unrelated to the company's present product/market scope (often associated with acquisitions).

Divestment　Refers to retrenchment strategy. The selling-off or liquidation of a division or unit of an organization.

Dividend　A proportion of the profits of a company which is distributed to the shareholders.

Dividend cover　Ratio between earnings per share and the ordinary dividend per share.

Dividend yield　Relationship between the ordinary dividend and the market price per ordinary share.

'Dodos'　Term for describing low share – negative growth products. Used in context of product life cycle/product portfolio analysis.

'Dogs'　Products which are at a cost disadvantage and have few opportunities for growth at a reasonable cost. Generally, low-market-share products needing cash to survive and, consequently, not profitable.

Earnings per share (EPS)　Net profit after tax attributable to the ordinary shareholders' dividend by the number of ordinary shares.

Earnings yield　Relationship between the earnings per ordinary share and the market price per ordinary share. The reciprocal of the price-earnings ratio multiplied by 100.

Environment　Generally refers to *external* forces affecting the organization. These may be classified under legal, social, political, economic, technological and market forces.

EPS　*see* Earnings per share

Equity share capital　Issued share capital which has unlimited rights to participate in the distribution either of dividends or of capital. In its narrowest definition refers to ordinary shares only.

Experience curve　A postulate that suggests that as the firm grows in size and experience it is able to reduce costs and improve productivity, for a given activity.

Financial ratios　Relationships among items in financial statements.

Fixed assets　Assets held for use in the business rather than for re-sale, e.g. plant and machinery, fixtures and fittings, property.

Fixed overheads   Financial overheads which generally remain constant over the usual range of activity.

Gearing   The relationship between ordinary shareholders' funds and long-term sources of funds carrying a fixed interest charge or dividend.

Goodwill   The difference between the valuation of a company as a whole and the value placed in tangible assets and liabilities. Usually highlighted when the company is being evaluated for, say, potential purchase.

HC   *see* Historical cost

Historical cost (HC)   The usual basis of valuation in published financial statements. Favoured because it is less subjective and more easily verifiable by an auditor.

Holding company   A company which controls a subsidiary company or companies.

Intangible assets   Assets such as goodwill, patents and trademarks.

Integration   Growth strategy characterized by the extension of the firm's business definition, i.e. vertical (forward and backward) integration. In this case the firm may integrate forwards, to assure control of distribution, or backwards, to safeguard supplies of raw materials.

Issued share capital   Part of the authorized share capital which has been issued. The amount of the issued capital must be disclosed in the published balance sheet.

Issue price   The price at which a share is issued. Since the issue may be at a premium or a discount, the issue price is not necessarily equal to the par value.

Liabilities   Monies owing by a company, which must be disclosed in the published balance sheet. For example:

- bank loans and overdrafts
- other loans
- amounts owing to subsidiary companies
- recommended dividend
- redeemed debentures
- creditors.

Liquid ratio   The ratio of current assets, minus stocks, to current liabilities.

Loan capital   Funds acquired by non-short-term borrowing from sources other than the shareholders of the company.

Long-term debt   Long-term sources of funds other than equity (share capital and reserves).

Market price   The price at which a company's shares can be bought or sold on a Stock Exchange at a particular time.

Minority interest   Part of a subsidiary company's shareholders' funds not held by the holding company. Usually shown as a separate item on the consolidated balance sheet.

Management buy out (MBO)   When the management of the company buy it from the owners.

Management information systems (MIS)   A formal system of gathering intelligence – information to be used by the strategist. For example, economic data, market reports, technological development, etc. plus data on internal operations.

MBO   *see* Management buy out

MIS   *see* Management information system

Net current assets   Same as working capital.

Net profit ratio   Ratio at net profit to sales.

Net tangible assets   Assets other than intangible assets, less liabilities.

Net worth   Assets less liabilities. The proprietorship section of a balance sheet, usually referred to in the case of a company as shareholders' funds or share capital and reserves.

Nominal share capital   Same as authorized share capital.

Non-voting shares   Shares carrying no voting rights. Usually cheaper to buy than those carrying votes.

Objectives   Desired targets or results which, at the basic level, may be expressed in financial, product/mission or social-psychological terms; at the fulfilling level, objectives may be defined in more directed fashion such as relationships with customers or continuous improvement of resources.

Ordinary shares   Shares entitled to share in the profits after payment of loan interest and preference dividends.

Paid-up share capital   The amount of the called-up share capital which has been paid up by the shareholders.

Par value   The face value of a share. Usually different from the issue price or the current market price. Dividend and interest percentages refer to the par value and yield to the current market price.

Payback   Payback is the time period for the outlay on an investment to be recovered.

PIMS   *see* Profit impact of market strategies

Profit impact of market strategies (PIMS)   US study relating to profitability analysis (see Schoeffler, Buzzell and Heany, 'Impact of Strategic Planning on Profit Performance', *Harvard Business Review*, Vol. 52, (March–April 1974, pp. 137–45)).

Policies   Broad guidelines to pursuing fulfilling objectives, and designed to clarify or sharpen up those objectives.

Preference shares   Shares which are normally entitled to a fixed rate of dividend prior to dividend payment on the ordinary shares. If a preference dividend is not paid, the arrears must be disclosed as a footnote to the balance sheet.

Price-Earnings ratio   The multiple of the last reported earnings per share that the market is willing to pay, for a company's ordinary share. The reciprocal of earnings yield multiplied by 100.

'Problem Children'   *see* Question marks

Product portfolio analysis   Relates to specific marketing strategies to achieve a balanced mix of products that will produce the maximum long-run effects from scarce cash and management resources.

'Question Marks'   Sometimes known as 'problem children'. High growth/low market-share products. Cash generation is low and cash needs high.

Quick ratio   The relationship between quickly realizable assets and current liabilities. Also known as liquid ratio, or the acid test. A measure of liquidity.

Quoted investments   Investments for which there is a quotation or permission to deal on a recognized Stock Exchange or on any reputable Stock Exchange outside Great Britain. Must be shown separately in the balance sheet.

Reserves   Represent the retention of profits or monies from specific capital transactions such as the issue of shares at a premium or the revaluation of assets.

Retained profits   Profits retained for re-investment in the company.

ROI   *see* Return on investment

Return on capital employed (ROCE)   Return on capital employed is profit before interest and tax as a percentage of capital employed.

Return on investment (ROI)   Profitability measurement which is the ratio of profit (usually before interest and tax) to net tangible assets.

Revaluation   The revaluation of an asset to its current market value.

Revenue reserves Reserves regarded by the directors as being normally available for dividend.

Rights issue An issue of shares where existing shareholders have the right to subscribe for the new share at a given price. The shareholder has the option to sell the right if unwilling to subscribe.

ROCE see Return on capital employed

SBU see Strategic business unit

Share capital If it is not limited by guarantee, a company registered under the Companies Act must have a share capital divided into a fixed amount. Ownership of a share gives the holder a proportionate ownership of the company.

Shareholder A member whose share in the company is evidenced by the holding of a share certificate.

Shareholders' funds The proprietorship section of a company balance sheet. Comprises the share capital and reserves.

Share premium Arises from issuing shares at a price higher than their par value. Can be used to make an issue of bonus shares, but not to pay dividends.

'Stars' Products that are market leaders and also growing at a fast rate. They represent the best opportunity for growth and investment.

Stocks and work-in-progress Consists (for a manufacturing company) of raw materials, work-in-progress and finished goods. Usually valued at the lower of cost or market value.

Stock turnover Ratio of sales or cost of sales to stocks.

Strategy As a concept, refers to the total system incorporating the firm's objectives, policies and the planning required to achieve objectives. In the managerial sense, strategy relates to the continuous process of effectively relating the organization's objectives and resources to opportunities in the environment.

Strategic business unit (SBU) An operating division of a firm which serves a distinct product-market segment or well-defined set of customers. Generally it has the authority to make its own strategic decisions as long as they meet corporate objectives.

Substitutes The extent to which competing products are substituted by buyers in the purchase process. Perfect substitutes are those with no perceptible differences. See cross-elasticity of demand.

Synergy Exists when the strengths of two companies or units when put together, more than off-set their joint weaknesses.

(a) Many products resulting in higher utilization of facilities, personnel and overhead (operating synergy).
(b) Many products using same plant and equipment (investment synergy).
(c) Management experience in one industry helping to solve problems in another industry (management synergy).

Synergy can thus be gained through application of production, marketing or financial expertise.

Times interest earned   The number of times that a company's interest is covered or earned by its profit before interest and tax.

Turnover   Relates to the sales of a company appearing in the profit and loss account.

Unquoted investments   Investments for which there is not a quotation or permission to deal on a recognized Stock Exchange or on any reputable Stock Exchange outside Great Britain. If they consist of equity of other companies, directors must either give an estimate of their value or information about income received, profits, etc.

Unsecured loan   Money borrowed by a company without the giving of security.

'War Horses'   Term used to describe high-share/negative growth products. Used in context of product life cycle/product portfolio analysis.

Working capital   Current assets less current liabilities.

Work-in-progress   Partly completed manufactured goods.

Index